The New Chicago Diner COOKBOOK

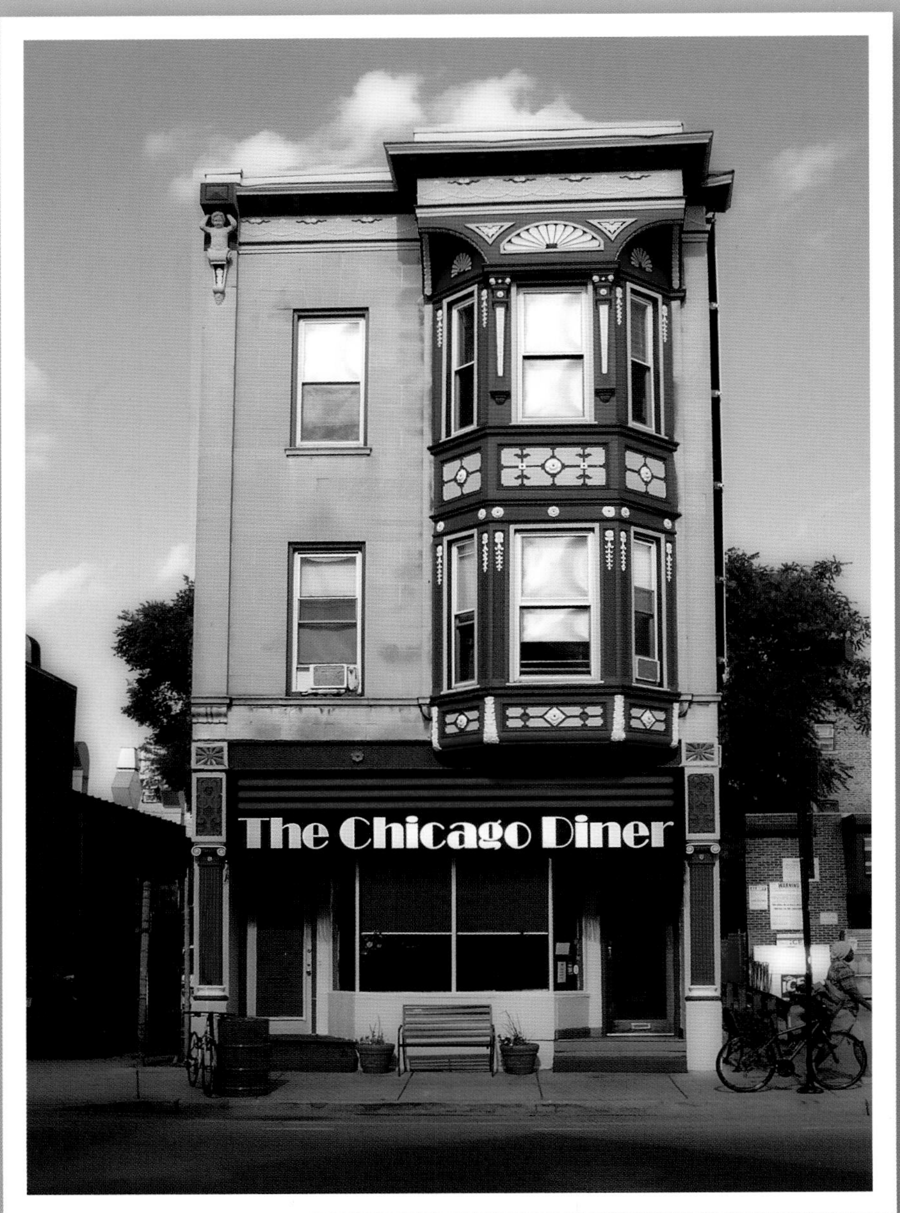
The Chicago Diner

The New Chicago Diner COOKBOOK

Meat-free recipes from America's veggie diner

Jo A. Kaucher with Kat Barry
& The Chicago Diner Crew

MIDWAY

AN AGATE IMPRINT

CHICAGO

Printed in Korea.

Library of Congress Cataloging-in-Publication Data

Kaucher, Jo A.,

The new Chicago Diner cookbook : meat-free recipes from America's veggie diner / by Jo A. Kaucher with Kat Barry and the Chicago Diner crew.

pages cm

Summary: "The second collection of recipes from The Chicago Diner, the city's premier vegetarian restaurant"-- Provided by publisher.

Includes index.

ISBN 978-1-57284-154-3 (paperback) -- ISBN 1-57284-154-0 (paperback)

1. Vegetarian cooking. 2. Chicago Diner. I. Barry, Kat. II. Kaucher, Jo A., 1952- Chicago Diner cookbook. III. Chicago Diner. IV. Title.

TX837.K2599 2013

641.5'636--dc23

2013031522

13 14 15 16 10 9 8 7 6 5 4 3 2 1

Midway is an imprint of Agate Publishing. Agate books are available in bulk at discount prices. For more information, go to agatepublishing.com.

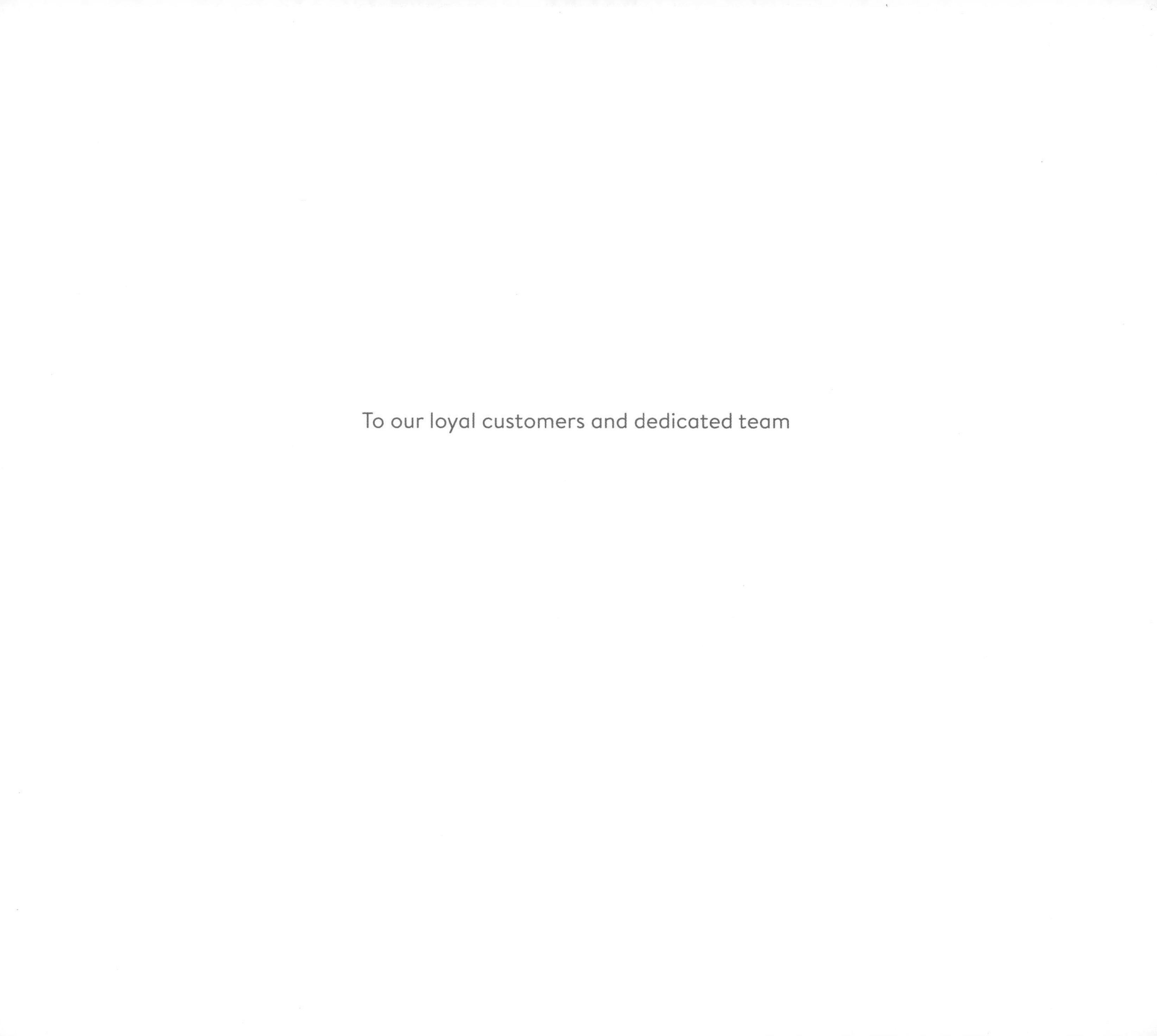

To our loyal customers and dedicated team

August 1982, pre-opening street fair

Contents

MEAT FREE
Since '83

Foreword

THE WAY A DINER SHOULD BE

"Meat free since '83" is the no-bones-about-it slogan of the Chicago Diner, an unassuming vegetarian haven in a city chock-full of meat eateries. Way back in 1983, the idea of serving classic diner fare without meat seemed absurd. That the Diner's tradition has withstood the test of time is a triumph of optimism, creativity, and tenacity. The Diner's menu sounds familiar: burgers, fries, and shakes—typical American comfort food, right? The twist: At the Diner, these classics are prepared with a side order of humanity.

Husband and wife cofounders Marshall "Mickey" Hornick and Chef Jo A. Kaucher first met in 1979, when they worked together at the Bread Shop Kitchen, a "granola and sprouts" health food eatery located at 3411 N. Halsted Street, Chicago, that had seen better days. They spent more than a year working together there, but by 1981, the Kitchen had run out of steam. The restaurant shut down, and the budding duo went their separate ways.

When he learned that Jo was leaving for California, Mickey pledged to her, "Someday I'll find you, wherever you are, and we'll open a restaurant together." At the time, Jo wasn't entirely convinced of his sincerity, but after a year living out West (coincidentally, she was Bob Dylan's next-door neighbor), she returned to the Windy City...and Mickey followed through on his promise.

Marshall "Mickey" Hornick and Jo A. Kaucher, Thanksgiving 1983

The location search for their new restaurant brought them to the verge of leasing a space next door to the beautiful Music Box Theater on Southport. But then the 3411 N. Halsted location, the place where they'd met a few years earlier, fortuitously became available at the last moment. There was something special about the place that just felt right. On April 2, 1983, the Chicago Diner opened in the historic "painted lady" edifice that it is known for today.

Jo, a self-taught chef with experience in many restaurant and hotel kitchens, drew upon her innate talent to create the menu from scratch. At age 19, she gave up meat on a lark; it turned out to be a lifelong commitment. In 1984, she was asked by notable

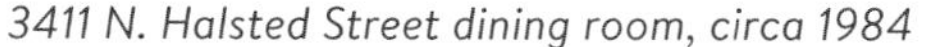

3411 N. Halsted Street dining room, circa 1984

vegetarian chef Ron Pickarski to join the sole vegan team in a field of 900 competitors in the International Culinary Olympics. They came away victorious, with two silver medals and a sense of pride and accomplishment.

As the decades passed, word spread about the veggie diner and vegetarianism in general. The Internet helped open people's eyes to new perspectives on health and diet, factory farming, and ecological sustainability. With good reasons, people were looking to eat less meat without feeling deprived. The Chicago Diner delivered meat-free comfort food, and then some.

At the end of 2012, on the cusp of The Chicago Diner's 30th anniversary, a second location in the Logan Square neighborhood opened to an enthusiastic reception. The 2333 N. Milwaukee Avenue location serves the same menu as the original Diner amidst a contemporary mix of reclaimed wood furnishings, local artwork, and stylish fixtures. The facility also boasts a LEED Gold green building certification, evidence of the Diner's mission to conduct business sustainably in a world with dwindling resources.

Both Chicago Diner locations share a spirit of warmth and kindness that perfectly compliments the comforting cuisine. Jo Kaucher's passion is evident in the food; the heart of the place is inspired by her other half, Mickey Hornick, an idealistic and hopeful dreamer, Chicago native, and devoted Cubs fan (as hopeful as dreamers get). Hornick's founding principle that "this is the way a diner should be" lives on

3411 N. Halsted Street dining room, circa 2010

to this day, and now the next generation is continuing the family tradition. Hornick's nephew, Michael, became manager of the restaurants in 2011.

Since 1983, vegetarianism's trickle has grown into a movement. American meat consumption is in decline. Environmental sustainability is increasingly a part of the collective consciousness. Riding this wave of progress, the Chicago Diner is still "meat free since '83" and going strong. This kind-hearted, eco-friendly diner and its hungry fans, both new and old, are keeping the dream alive.

The Chicago Diner
LOGAN SQUARE

Recipes for Success

Over the years, the Chicago Diner has developed a reputation for surprising and delighting visitors, including skeptics and passersby who were drawn in by the promise of diner food. In the old days, a patron might stroll in, take a seat, spend a moment looking at the menu, and then head for the door...with urgency, as if caught in a strange alternate universe. Eventually, word got out that something innovative and delicious was happening, and there were plenty of folks who were eager to embrace the concept.

Fast forward a few decades. The Chicago Diner has become an internationally recognized mecca for vegetarian dining, a landmark visited by travelers from around the globe. They join the throngs of locals who also have a fond attachment to the Diner's unique brand of food. In response to countless customer requests to revisit dishes from the past, *The Chicago Diner Cookbook* was published in 2002 and featured selected recipes from the Diner's first two decades.

The New Chicago Diner Cookbook is an all-new collection of favorites, popular stand-outs, and timeless classics. The book picks up where the previous book left off. The recipes are all plant-based (vegan) and cover a range of skill levels. As your experience with plant-based cooking grows, the book has more to offer you.

Many of the recipes are customer and staff favorites that are practical enough to make at home, starting with the basics of vegan cooking. Naturally, the ever popular Radical Reuben™ and the secrets to the Diner's amazing "corned beef," bacun, and other signature meat substitutes are included, too.

There is also practicality built into the collection: Some of the recipes are reused and combined in different ways to form multiple dishes. This efficiency will leave more time to spend with family and friends, while spending less money at the grocery store. With a foundation of vegan cooking basics plus guidance in mixing and matching dishes, you'll have the confidence to explore your creativity and step outside the recipe.

Use this book as a primer and an inspirational tool for exploring veganism with your loved ones. After all, what's more inspiring than creating the magic of the Chicago Diner in your home?

Thank you for veggie dining!

—Del Nakamura

DIRECTOR OF MARKETING, THE CHICAGO DINER

Introduction

PANTRY ESSENTIALS FOR A VEGAN KITCHEN

Cooking well can be achieved by keeping it simple. It doesn't need to be complicated or have exotic ingredients but it all starts with the basics. Following is a list of essentials for the modern vegan home kitchen. Some of these items will inspire even the most novice cook, and others will further educate well-versed cooks who are new to vegan cuisine. No matter which category you fall into, always remember to be creative but keep it simple.

ESSENTIAL TOOLS OF THE TRADE

KNIVES: Your first three knives should be a paring knife, chef's knife, and serrated knife or trimmer (for breads and tomatoes). Quality, sharp knives that feel good in your hand are absolutely necessary, both for ease and for safety. Knives can be pricey, so plan to buy just three decent knives as a preliminary step; you can always build from there. Discount stores as well as kitchen supply stores often sell three-packs of quality knives.

CUTTING BOARDS: Wood should be used only for bread. For all other foods, stick with plastic; just replace when worn or when it begins to show knife cuts. Glass boards look nice, but they dull your knives and can be dangerous.

POTS AND PANS: Just as with the knives, there are three key pots and pans you should have on hand: a frying pan, saucepan, and stockpot. And in our opinion, no kitchen is complete without a cast-iron skillet. Consider picking one up at a thrift store or yard sale if you're on a tight budget. Even one covered in rust will clean up in a jiffy with some steel wool. Once the rust is gone, apply a coating of oil and get cooking.

BASIC KITCHEN TOOLS:

- Potato peeler
- Metal and silicone whisks
- Stainless and glass mixing bowls in a variety of sizes
- Liquid and dry measuring cups
- Hand juicer
- Two baking sheets (or one baking sheet and parchment paper, for easy cleanups and reuse)
- 9 × 13-inch (22.5 × 32.5-cm) and 9 × 9-inch (22.5 × 22.5-cm) baking dishes
- Large metal, wooden, and nylon (for nonstick cookware) spoons
- Tongs
- Spatula
- Pot holders and towels
- Thin rubber scraper
- Colander, for draining and washing
- Kitchen shears: They have tons of uses! The better they are, the more you'll find yourself using them.

MORE ADVANCED TOOLS:

- Garlic press
- Blender
- Hand mixer
- Stand mixer
- Food processor
- More knives
- Mesh strainer
- Salad spinner
- Rolling pin
- Pastry mat
- Muffin tins

PANTRY PARTICULARS

"The modern-day spoiled chef wants everything... All you need is salt, pepper, a cutting board, a good knife, lemons, and parsley." —**CHEF JO**

ORGANIC: We recommend shopping for organic produce as much as your budget will allow. When you have to make a choice, check the Internet for the latest "dirty dozen" list of the most pesticide contaminated produce. Also, check your nearest farmers' market for locally sourced organic produce. It's very comforting to know who grows your food and where it comes from.

BEANS: Both dried and canned are great to have on hand. You should also keep one can or bag of: lentils, split peas, red beans, black beans, garbanzo beans, and cannellini or other white beans.

NUTS AND SEEDS: Try to stock walnuts, sesame seeds, sunflower seeds, pecans, almonds, flaxseeds, and cashews in your pantry. We recommend using raw, unsalted nuts so you can do more with them. Store them in the refrigerator and/or freezer once they're opened. Nuts and seeds have a lot of oils in them and can become rancid.

OILS: We recommend keeping coconut (especially for baking cookies and bars), extra virgin olive (watch the temperature—olive oil burns easily), toasted sesame (mix with a less expensive oil to make a little go a long way), vegetable, and grapeseed oil, as well as a vegan margarine (we like trans-fat free Earth Balance), as it's a great substitute for butter.

BREADS: You should have regular wheat bread, pita bread, and tortillas on hand. We really like the Ezekiel brand, because it contains less sugar and offers a variety of healthy options. Always opt for 100% whole grain, the healthiest choice.

NUTRITIONAL YEAST: "Nooch" makes everything better! It tastes kind of cheesy and is rich in Vitamin B-12. It's great for thickening up sauces and sprinkling on pretty much anything savory! You may find it at Whole Foods Market or a health food store.

FLOURS: You should have all-purpose, whole wheat, and rice flour. It's a good idea to keep cornmeal and gluten-free flour mix too.

UNBLEACHED, NATURAL SWEETENERS: In most of our recipes, we recommend organic granulated cane sugar. We use Florida Crystals because it is vegan (not all brands are). But there's also agave nectar, palm, coconut, maple syrup, brown rice syrup, and molasses to sweeten things up.

GRAINS: Keep stocks of rice, bulgur, millet, quinoa (actually, it's a seed), barley, wild rice, couscous, corn grits (polenta), and oats (both quick-cooking and rolled). Make sure to store in airtight containers.

PASTA AND SAUCE: You're ready for anything if you have whole wheat noodles, quinoa pasta, soba noodles, rice noodles, linguine, and lasagna noodles in your cupboard. Making your own sauce is easy, but it's great to have a back-up plan (i.e. jarred sauce) for when you're extra rushed. Avoid any that contain high fructose corn syrup.

PLANT-BASED MILKS: Almond, soy, and coconut are all good options. Most soy milks have added oil, so be sure to read the ingredients. Coconut milk has a whole milk consistency that's nice for baking.

DRIED FRUITS: Any and all! These are great for making trail mix, healthy snacking, baking, and adding to savory dishes.

DRIED HERBS AND SPICES: This is quite a list, but they're all very important: sea salt, black pepper, bay leaves, vegetable bouillon cubes, basil, parsley, oregano, garlic powder, onion, dill, ground mustard, turmeric, cayenne pepper, cumin, paprika (plain and smoked), chili powder, herbes de Provence, and Italian seasoning or other mixed blends. (Mixed herb blends and seasoning salts really come in handy, especially when you're first learning what flavors pair well.) We also recommend having sage, rosemary, white pepper, and thyme in your pantry.

VINEGARS: Balsamic, apple cider, white wine, red wine, and rice vinegar should round out your collection. White wine vinegar is particularly nice for baking because it's a little sweeter. Plain white vinegar also doubles as an effective and safe household cleaner.

CANNED GOODS: Keep tomatoes (whole or crushed), tomato paste, vegetarian refried beans, pineapple, Thai coconut milk, and sundried tomatoes in your pantry. You can also buy canned vegetable broth, but you'll stop once you realize how easy and cheap it is to make your own!

CONDIMENTS: Essentials include tamari, soy sauce, organic ketchup, prepared mustard, vegan mayonnaise, vegan Worcestershire sauce, hot sauce, mirin, jam, jelly, natural nut butters like peanut and almond, salsa, pickles, and olives. You can make a lot of these yourself as your skills progress. If you buy premade versions, be sure to carefully read the labels.

MEAT ANALOGS: We do apply meat-centric names like "steak" or "chicken" to plant-based proteins, but don't let that make you think that they're "fake" foods. Tofu, tempeh, and seitan are made from beans and grains. They are real foods that taste great and add a satisfying heartiness to vegan dishes. Especially for kids or a traditional "meat and potatoes" type of American, meat analogs are a good way to transition to eating less meat without feeling deprived.

BAKING ESSENTIALS: Baking powder, baking soda, cornstarch and/or arrowroot powder, egg replacers (see p. 151 for more detail), pure vanilla extract, ground cinnamon, cacao powder, ground ginger, pumpkin pie spice, cloves, and nutmeg.

STOCK YOUR FREEZER: Frozen produce can be more nutritious than fresh in the grocery store, since they are frozen very soon after harvesting. It's often more convenient, too. Stock up on produce when it's in season and freeze for the winter. Of course, frozen is not appropriate for all dishes. You can try co-op or farmers' markets for the freshest local harvest. It's also a good idea to freeze veggie burgers, homemade vegetable stock, and at least one homemade ready-to-go meal.

FRESH PRODUCE THAT MAKES LIFE EASIER: carrots, apples, bananas, celery, leafy greens (chard, bok choy, kale, collards), peppers (bell, sweet, and hot), fresh parsley and at least one other herb (such as cilantro or basil), arugula, lemons, cabbage (red or green), any variety of lettuce, mushrooms, potatoes, tomatoes, onion, and garlic.

Vegan Proteins and Fillings

One of the myths about meatless diets is that they're deficient in protein. In this section, you will learn how to make some basic staples that are protein-rich alternatives to meat. You will come up with countless ways to use these building-block recipes. Make extra for salads, sandwiches, or a main dish. Preparing these in advance will help you be a healthy veggie on the go.

PICTURED: **Marinated Portobello Mushrooms (p. 26)**

Herb-Citrus Tofu

This is a really light and simple tofu marinade that can be used in a variety of recipes. Once it sits for a while in this wonderful marinade, you can grill or bake the tofu and slice it up for sandwiches, use it as a hearty topping for salads, or pair it with greens and grains for a balanced meal. The options are endless! Keep some delicious baked or grilled tofu in the fridge all the time, so you can throw together a healthy meal in a flash.

YIELD: **16 ounces marinade (enough for 2 [12-ounce or 341-g] packages extra-firm tofu)**

- **2 cups (474 mL) water**
- **1 clove garlic, minced**
- **1 vegetable bouillon cube**
- **½ teaspoon dried thyme**
- **½ teaspoon dried rosemary**
- **½ teaspoon freshly ground black pepper**
- **Zest and juice of 1 lemon**
- **2 (12-ounce [341-g]) packages extra-firm tofu**

1. In a large stockpot over medium–high heat, place all of the ingredients except the tofu. Bring to a boil. Reduce heat and simmer for 10 minutes. Remove from the heat and set aside.

2. Strain the marinade and chill it in the refrigerator for 1 hour.

3. When the marinade has cooled completely, place the tofu in a large, shallow baking dish and cover it with the marinade. Cover the dish and refrigerate overnight. Halfway through the marinating time, turn the tofu once and cover it again with the marinade, if necessary.

4. (If baking) Preheat the oven to 350°F (150°C). (If grilling) Preheat the grill on high heat.

5. (If baking) Bake for 20 minutes. Remove from the oven. (If grilling) Place on the grill for 10 to 15 minutes, turning once halfway through the grilling time. Remove from the heat. Serve immediately or store in an airtight container in the refrigerator for 5 to 7 days.

COOKS' NOTE: if you don't have bouillon cubes, use 1½ teaspoons sea salt.

Hickory-Marinated Tempeh

This recipe is a staple! Tempeh is a fantastic meat substitute made from fermented soybeans. It can be crumbled to resemble sausage, perhaps as a pizza topping or in a casserole; cut into strips for fajitas; or cubed. Really, the sky's the limit with this one. But remember—the key with tempeh is in making sure it's fully cooked.

YIELD: Marinade for 1 (12-ounce [341-g]) package tempeh

- ¾ cup (178 mL) water
- ¼ cup (59 mL) Vegan Worcestershire Sauce (see recipe on p. 90 or try the Wizard brand)
- 3 tablespoons (45 mL) Bragg's Liquid Aminos or soy sauce
- 1 tablespoon liquid smoke
- 1–2 teaspoons Sriracha sauce (optional)
- 1½ teaspoons garlic powder
- 1½ teaspoons onion powder
- 1 teaspoon sea salt
- 1 (12-ounce [341-g]) package raw tempeh
- ½ tablespoon canola or grapeseed oil

1. In a large mixing bowl, whisk together all the ingredients except the tempeh and oil.

2. Cut the tempeh into sticks, cubes, or crumbles. Place them in a medium, shallow baking dish.

3. Pour the marinade over the tempeh. Cover and let sit at least 30 minutes. Refrigerate if you will be marinating for longer than 30 minutes.

4. In a large nonstick skillet over medium heat, warm the oil. Add the tempeh to the skillet and pan fry for 5 minutes, until golden brown on all sides. Remove from the heat. Serve immediately or store in an airtight container in the refrigerator for 5 to 7 days.

Diner Seitan

Seitan is made from the protein part of wheat (gluten). It has a very convincing meatlike texture and is the most popular meat substitute among our customers. It's not the easiest thing to make from scratch, but it freezes well and the awesomeness of a homemade Radical Reuben can't be beat! Seitan is versatile, a good source of iron, high in protein, and low in fat and carbs. Unfortunately, some are sensitive to or intolerant of gluten, but for the rest of us, seitan is a tasty lean "meat" that works wonders.

YIELD: **2 pounds (908 g) seitan**

- **4 cups (906 g) vital wheat gluten**
- **¾ cup (101 g) whole wheat flour**
- **3 tablespoons (42 g) nutritional yeast flakes**
- **2 tablespoons onion powder**
- **2 tablespoons mixed dried herbs (your choice; we recommend Frontier brand)**
- **1½ tablespoons celery salt**
- **½ tablespoon garlic powder**
- **1 teaspoon white pepper (optional)**
- **2¼ cups (533 mL) warm water**
- **¼ cup (59 mL) soy sauce**
- **2 cups (300 g) chopped vegetables (use the same variety you'd use to make stock)**
- **3 whole cloves garlic**
- **3 or 4 bay leaves**

1. In the bowl of a stand mixer fitted with the paddle attachment, combine the gluten, flour, nutritional yeast, onion powder, herbs, celery salt, garlic powder, and white pepper (if using). Mix on low speed until well combined.

2. Add the water and soy sauce to the bowl. Mix on low speed until well combined.

3. Remove the paddle attachment and replace it with the dough hook attachment. Mix with the dough hook attachment on low speed for 10 to 15 minutes, kneading the mixture until it looks like dough.

4. Knead for 10 more minutes, until the mixture pulls away from the sides of the bowl.

5. Remove the bowl from the mixer and cover it with a towel. Allow the dough to rest for 15 minutes at room temperature.

6. Remove the dough from the bowl. Place on a cutting board. Cut the dough in half, and then again into fourths.

7. In a large stockpot containing 1 gallon (3.8 L) of water, place the pieces of dough, chopped vegetables, garlic cloves, and bay leaves. The pot should be large enough to accommodate the dough as it triples in size once cooked. Turn the heat to medium-high. Bring to a boil. Reduce the heat to medium-low.

8. Allow the seitan to simmer for 1½ hours, until the seitan triples in size. Remove from the heat. Remove and discard the bay leaves, vegetables, and garlic.

9. Remove the seitan from the stockpot. Inspect it carefully to ensure that it is firm and not sticky.

10. Place the seitan in a large, deep baking dish. Cover it with cold water and a splash of soy sauce. Store it in the refrigerator until it has fully cooled.

11. Once the seitan has fully cooled, remove it from the water and slice, dice, or grind it (and marinate it) according to your recipe plans.

COOKS' NOTE: You can store prepared seitan covered in water in an airtight container in the refrigerator for up to 2 weeks or in the freezer for up to 3 months.

Bacun, Italian-Style, and Corned "Beef" Marinated Seitan

YIELD: **2 cups (474 mL) marinade**

For a Bacun Marinade:

- **1 cup (237 mL) water**
- **¼ cup (59 mL) liquid smoke**
- **¼ cup (59 mL) soy sauce**
- **1 teaspoon sea salt**
- **2 dashes A-1 Sauce or Vegan Worcestershire Sauce (see recipe on p. 90)**

For an Italian-Style Marinade:

- **1½ cups (356 mL) water**
- **¼ cup (59 mL) vegetable oil**
- **¼ cup (59 mL) soy sauce**
- **1½ tablespoons onion powder**
- **1 tablespoon garlic powder**
- **1 teaspoon dried basil**
- **1 teaspoon dried oregano**
- **1 bay leaf**

For a Corned "Beef" Marinade:

- **1 cup (237 mL) pickle juice**
- **¾ cup (178 mL) beet juice (juice from a jar of pickled beets works fine)**
- **1½ teaspoons garlic powder**
- **1½ teaspoons onion powder**
- **½ teaspoon caraway seed**
- **½ teaspoon dried dill weed**
- **¼ teaspoon fennel seed**
- **Dash dry ground mustard**
- **Freshly ground black pepper, to taste**

To make each of the Marinades:

1. In a large mixing bowl, mix all of the ingredients together until fully combined.

2. Slice the seitan thinly. Place it in a large, shallow baking dish. Pour the marinade over the seitan and marinate in the refrigerator for 1 to 2 days.

3. Pan fry, sauté, bake, or grill the seitan according to your recipe plans.

VARIATION: You can also use the Diner's Red Pepper Sauce (see recipe on p. 121) as a marinade for spicy Asian-style dishes or our Hickory Tempeh Sauce (see recipe on p. 21) as a marinade with a smoky flavor.

VARIATION: For Chickun-Style Seitan, use chickpea flour instead of whole wheat, omit the soy sauce, add 2 to 3 teaspoons sea salt, and use 1 tablespoon poultry spice and 1 tablespoon dried parsley instead of the 2 tablespoons mixed dried herbs.

Blackened Tofu

Tofu is one of those ingredients that can be used in so many ways, it should have its own cookbook. Many people write tofu off as not really having much flavor, but it really holds its own when coated in blackened spices. Grill or bake these tofu slices and serve them as a tofu steak in an entrée, slice them up for a sandwich, or cube them for a salad.

YIELD: **12 ounces (341 g) Blackened Tofu**

- 1 (12-ounce [341-g]) package extra-firm tofu
- 1 tablespoon ground paprika (smoked or plain)
- 2 teaspoons freshly ground black pepper
- 1–2 teaspoons ground cayenne pepper
- 1 teaspoon sea salt
- 1 teaspoon garlic powder
- 1 teaspoon onion powder
- 1 teaspoon dried oregano
- 1 teaspoon dried thyme
- ¼ teaspoon ground nutmeg
- 1½ teaspoons Ener-G Egg Replacer
- 2 tablespoons water
- ½ teaspoon agave nectar

1. Unwrap the package of tofu and place it on a plate lined with paper towels to drain for 1 hour.

2. In a large, shallow dish, mix together the paprika, black pepper, cayenne pepper, salt, garlic powder, onion powder, oregano, thyme, and nutmeg, creating your "blackened" seasoning. Set aside.

3. Preheat the oven to 350°F (180°C). Lightly grease a baking sheet.

4. Slice the narrower plane of the tofu in half. Stack the 2 halves and slice it again down the center, resulting in 4 slices of tofu that are half the thickness of the original block. Place the tofu slices on a dinner plate.

5. In a small mixing bowl, whisk together the egg replacer, water, and agave nectar. Brush each side of each tofu slice with the egg replacer–agave mixture.

6. Dip each slice of tofu in the seasoning spices, turning to coat each side thoroughly.

7. Place the tofu slices on the prepared baking sheet. Bake for 25 minutes. Remove from the oven.

COOKS' NOTE: Egg replacer works really well as a binding agent and is a nice alternative to cornstarch.

Tofu Ricotta

This is a very useful and versatile recipe to have in your repertoire. It's a quick, delicious, and healthy homemade cheese substitute that's perfect in pasta dishes, as a topping for pizza, as a stuffing for lasagna and shells, or even as a salad all on its own.

YIELD: **4 cups (908 g)**

- 1 (12-ounce [341-g]) package extra-firm tofu, drained and crumbled
- ½ cup (76 g) chopped white onion
- 1½ teaspoons sea salt, divided
- 4 cloves garlic, minced
- 2–3 cups (60–90 g) finely chopped fresh spinach
- ¼ cup (6 g) finely chopped fresh basil
- ¼ cup (56 g) nutritional yeast flakes
- 2 tablespoons extra virgin olive oil
- 2 teaspoons fresh lemon juice
- 1 teaspoon dried oregano
- ¼ teaspoon freshly ground black pepper

1. Place the crumbled tofu in a large mixing bowl.

2. In a small mixing bowl, combine the onion with ½ teaspoon of the salt. Massage the salt into the onion pieces with your hands to "salt cook" the onion. Add the garlic and massage together again.

3. Add the contents of the small mixing bowl to the large mixing bowl. Add all the remaining ingredients. With clean hands, mash the mixture together thoroughly. Use immediately in your favorite recipe or store in an airtight container in the refrigerator for up to 1 week.

COOKS' NOTE: The consistency of your ricotta should depend on what you're using it for. If you need it to have a smoother texture, don't mash the mixture with your hands; instead, pulse everything except the spinach and basil in the bowl of a food processor fitted with the metal "S" blade until it is smooth. Then, add the spinach and basil, pulse a couple more times, and transfer the ricotta to a bowl or into your recipe.

VARIATION: This recipe is also great with kale instead of spinach, especially if you refrigerate it overnight (thus allowing the kale leaves to soften a bit).

Marinated Portobello Mushrooms

Portobello mushrooms are a popular ingredient in vegetarian cuisine due to their meaty and hearty texture. They also offer the familiar rich, heavy flavors many became used to when they had a meat-based diet. This marinade is a great go-to for all kinds of mushrooms and for the variety of ways you can prepare them. Use these on sandwiches, salads, pasta dishes, or feature in a main dish.

YIELD: **1 pound (454 g) marinated mushrooms; 2 cups (474 mL) marinade**

- **½ cup (119 mL) balsamic vinegar**
- **½ cup (119 mL) extra virgin olive oil**
- **4 cloves garlic, minced**
- **2 teaspoons fresh lemon juice**
- **1 teaspoon dried parsley**
- **1 teaspoon dried basil**
- **1 pound (454 g) whole portobello mushrooms**

1. In a medium mixing bowl, whisk together all of the ingredients except the mushrooms.

2. Clean mushrooms by carefully brushing with a soft bristle brush, if you have one, or rinsing them under running water. Pat dry. Slice or leave whole depending on how you are going to prepare them (see step 5 and the Cooks' Notes).

3. Add the mushrooms to the bowl. Toss the mushrooms with the marinade until evenly coated.

4. Cover the mixing bowl and refrigerate for 6 to 8 hours, or overnight. Stir the mixture once or twice during the marinating time.

5. Sauté, grill, or bake the mushrooms (see Cooks' Notes). Add them to your favorite dish or serve with side dishes as an entrée.

COOKS' NOTES: To sauté the mushrooms, warm 1 teaspoon of olive oil in a large skillet over medium heat. Slice up the mushrooms. Add the mushrooms to the skillet and sauté for 10 minutes, until they become tender.

To grill the mushrooms, place the whole mushroom caps on a sheet of foil on the top rack of a grill set on medium heat for 20 minutes, turning once throughout.

To bake the mushrooms, place them whole or sliced in a large casserole or cast iron skillet bathed in the marinade. Bake at 375°F (190°C) for 20 minutes. (You can also skewer them on kabobs; let your creativity be your guide!)

Use any leftover marinade as a salad dressing or toss it with other veggies and repeat the process.

VARIATION: For a lighter, oil-free version, substitute water instead of the olive oil.

Brunch

At the Chicago Diner, we think that brunch is arguably the best meal of the day. It's sort of an anything-goes type of meal. You can have anything you want, including a cocktail before (or shortly after) noon.

The time of day when brunch is served implies a certain ease. If you're having brunch, you've got the day off and plenty of time to enjoy the pleasures of good food and good company.

PICTURED: **Tofu Scramble (p. 29)**
Biscuits and White Sage Gravy (p. 40)

Breakfast Chorizo

Who doesn't love spicy savory crumbles atop their Tofu Scramble (see recipe on p. 29)? You can season seitan in a variety of ways to come up with some scrumptiously satisfying breakfast "meats" without the cruelty and cholesterol of their traditional counterparts.

YIELD: **1 pound (454 g)**

- **1 (1-pound [454-g]) package or homemade seitan**
- **½ tablespoon ground plain paprika**
- **½ tablespoon ground cumin**
- **½ teaspoon garlic powder**
- **½ teaspoon sea salt**
- **¼ teaspoon red pepper flakes**
- **Dash ancho chili powder**

1. Preheat the oven to 325°F (160°C). Lightly grease a baking sheet.

2. In the bowl of a food processor fitted with the metal "S" blade, add the seitan and pulse for 1 to 2 minutes, until the seitan reaches the consistency of ground chorizo.

3. In a large mixing bowl, combine all the spices. Use a whisk to mix them thoroughly. Toss the seitan and spices together.

4. Place the spiced seitan on the prepared baking sheet and bake for 10 minutes. Remove from the oven. Serve immediately or store in an airtight container in the refrigerator for up to 2 weeks.

VARIATION: For breakfast sausage flavor, substitute ¼ teaspoon dried thyme for the paprika, ¼ teaspoon fennel seed for the cumin, and ¼ teaspoon dried sage for the chili powder. You can even add a teaspoon of agar powder to give you the consistency needed to form the mixture into patties for pan frying.

Tofu Scramble

A great alternative to eggs, a good scrambled tofu can power your day. Several different versions have been featured at the Diner over the years. Here's the most current rendition of this veggie staple, from our kitchen to yours.

YIELD: **4 servings**

- 1 (12-ounce [341-g]) package extra-firm tofu
- 1 clove garlic, minced
- 2 tablespoons nutritional yeast flakes or tahini paste (optional)
- 1 teaspoon dried basil
- ½ teaspoon sea salt
- ¼ teaspoon ground turmeric
- ¼ teaspoon onion powder
- 1 tablespoon canola or grapeseed oil, for cooking

1. Unwrap the package of tofu and place it on a plate lined with paper towels to drain for 1 hour.

2. In a medium mixing bowl, using your clean hands, a fork, or a heavy whisk, crumble the tofu.

3. In a small mixing bowl, combine the garlic, nutritional yeast flakes (if using), basil, salt, turmeric, and onion powder.

4. Transfer the mixed spices into the medium mixing bowl. Using your clean hands, mix together the spices and tofu until the tofu is evenly and fully coated.

5. In a large skillet over medium–low heat, warm the oil. Add the tofu and sauté for 3 to 5 minutes. Remove from the heat. Serve immediately.

VARIATIONS: Like it better baked? You can also make Baked Tofu by baking the recipe on a lightly greased baking sheet for 10 to 12 minutes at 325°F (160°C).

Turn this into a Veggie Tofu Scramble by sautéing 2 cups (300 g) seasonal veggies in the pan before you add the tofu. At the end, toss in ¼ cup (8 g) fresh parsley. The result is a scrumptious skillet-style breakfast scramble.

Eating tempeh is a great way to incorporate fermented foods into your diet! Substitute pan-fried tempeh for the tofu in this dish by cooking the tempeh in ¼ cup (59 mL) Vegan Worcestershire Sauce (see recipe on p. 90), a few dashes of liquid smoke, and ½ tablespoon tamari.

Vegan Fried "Egg"

Thank goodness for this fried tofu patty, because it makes vegan breakfast sandwiches a delicious reality. Serve this delight atop biscuits or an English muffin for a veg Benedict, or stuff it between two French toast slices to create a vegan Monte Cristo.

YIELD: **4 patties (2 cups [454 g])**

- 1 (12-ounce [341-g]) package extra-firm tofu
- 2 tablespoons cornstarch
- ¼ cup water
- 2 tablespoons unbleached organic all-purpose or rice flour
- 1½ tablespoons nutritional yeast flakes
- 1½ tablespoons soy sauce
- 2 tablespoons vegetable oil, divided
- 1 teaspoon ground turmeric
- ½ teaspoon onion powder
- ½ teaspoon sea salt

1. Unwrap the package of tofu and place it on a plate lined with paper towels to drain for 1 hour.

2. In a small mixing bowl, whisk together the cornstarch and water. Set aside.

3. In the bowl of a food processor fitted with the metal "S" blade, crumble the tofu. Add the flour, the nutritional yeast flakes, the soy sauce, 1 tablespoon of the oil, the ground turmeric, the onion powder, and the sea salt.

4. Start the food processor and allow it to run. Slowly add in the cornstarch and water slurry. Blend until smooth. Transfer the mixture to a large pourable container.

5. In a large skillet or a griddle over medium heat, warm the remaining oil. Pour the mixture in ½-cup (119-mL) amounts onto the pan. Cook for 3 minutes on each side until browned on both sides, as you would a pancake. Serve immediately.

VARIATION: To recreate the Chicago Diner Monte Cristo, sandwich this fried egg inside French Toast (see recipe on p. 38), with Chickun and Bacun-Style Sliced Seitan (see recipe on pp. 22–23), your favorite vegan cheese and a dollop of Creole Remoulade Sauce (see recipe on p. 103).

Spicy Grits

Grits are a stick-to-your-ribs breakfast cereal, and spicy foods help kickstart your metabolism. This recipe is a great way to heat up a windy Chicago morning.

YIELD: **4 (½-cup [80-g]) servings**

- 3 cups (711 mL) water
- 1⅓ cups (213 g) yellow corn grits
- 1 tablespoon vegan margarine (we like Earth Balance) or extra virgin olive oil
- ½ teaspoon onion powder
- ½ teaspoon sea salt
- ¼–½ teaspoon ground cayenne pepper, or to taste
- Dash chili powder
- Freshly ground black pepper, to taste
- Sliced scallions and/or avocado, for garnish

1. In a large saucepan over medium–high heat, bring the water to a boil. While stirring constantly to avoid clumps, slowly pour the grits in.

2. Reduce the heat to a simmer and cook for 5 to 10 minutes, stirring occasionally to prevent sticking. (You want the grits to be about the same consistency as oatmeal, so keep that in mind and adjust the cooking time accordingly.)

3. Add the margarine, onion powder, salt, cayenne pepper, chili powder, and black pepper. Stir well. Remove from the heat. Serve immediately garnished with the scallions and/or avocado.

VARIATIONS: In summer, this dish is great with fresh, local hot peppers. Add 1 to 2 chopped jalapeño peppers, cayenne peppers, or whatever hot peppers you have access to in with this recipe. Remember: The longer you cook the peppers, the less hot they will be. Removing the seeds will also help reduce their heat. It's always wise to wear gloves when preparing hot peppers, as the oils can penetrate your skin and linger for hours.

To add even more flavor, you can stir in ½ cup (28 g) crumbled bacun, Chorizo (see recipe on p. 28), or corn niblets.

For Southern-Style Cheesy Grits, add ¼ cup (29 g) vegan cheddar cheese (such as Teese), ¼ cup (56 g) nutritional yeast flakes, and 1 cup (237 mL) soy or almond milk.

Great Lakes Zucchini Bread

Zucchini squash are plentiful in our region, so all Midwesterners must have several creative "zuc" dishes in their repertoire. Making a sweet breakfast bread out of a green vegetable seems like a great way to eat your veggies!

YIELD: **2 8½ x 4-inch (22 × 10-cm) loaves**

- **Vegan margarine, for greasing**
- **3 cups (405 g) whole wheat flour**
- **1¼ cups (250 g) organic granulated cane sugar**
- **1 tablespoon poppyseeds**
- **2½ teaspoons ground cinnamon**
- **1 teaspoon baking soda**
- **½ teaspoon sea salt**
- **3 tablespoons (42 g) milled flaxseed (see flaxseed baking instructions on p. 151)**
- **½ cup (119 mL) water**
- **½ cup (119 mL) agave nectar**
- **½ cup (119 mL) canola oil**
- **½ cup (119 mL) natural applesauce**
- **2 cups (248 g) shredded zucchini**
- **½ cup (55g) chopped pecans or walnuts**

1. Preheat the oven to 350°F (180°C). Prepare 2 8½ × 4-inch (22 × 10-cm) loaf pans by lightly greasing them with the margarine.

2. In a large mixing bowl, sift together the flour, sugar, poppyseeds, cinnamon, baking soda, and salt. Make a well in the center of the mixture and set aside.

3. In a small mixing bowl, whisk together the milled flaxseed and water. Add the agave nectar, oil, and applesauce.

4. Pour the wet ingredients into the bowl containing the dry ingredients. Stir well. (Be sure to scrape the sides of the bowl to make sure all the dry ingredients are thoroughly mixed.)

5. When the mixture is fully combined, fold in the zucchini. Next, fold in the nuts.

6. Spread equal amounts of the batter for the bread into each prepared pan. Bake for 40 minutes, until a cake tester inserted into the center of the loaf comes out clean. Remove from the oven. Serve immediately or store in an airtight container at room temperature for up to 5 days.

VARIATION: Transform this recipe into kid-friendly Chocolate Zucchini Bread by folding in 1 cup (180 g) dairy-free semisweet chocolate or carob chips at the very end of the batter mixing process.

Chicago Diner Pancakes

When you first choose a vegan lifestyle, it can be tough to imagine how to make certain things without eggs. This basic vegan pancake recipe is designed to show you that it's really quite simple. Top these yummy cakes with fruit, toss in nuts or dairy-free semisweet chocolate chips, or even change the wheat flour to cornmeal for a more savory preparation. Once you get the knack of making pancakes, there is really no limit to what you can do.

YIELD: **4–6 pancakes**

- 1¼ cups (151 g) unbleached organic all-purpose flour
- 2 tablespoons organic granulated cane sugar
- 1½ teaspoons baking powder
- 1½ teaspoons baking soda
- 1 teaspoon ground cinnamon
- ½ teaspoon sea salt
- 1–1¼ cups (237–296 mL) nut milk (any kind works!)
- ⅓ cup (79 mL) water
- 1 cup (166 g) fresh or frozen and thawed berries (optional)
- ½ tablespoon vegetable oil
- Maple Whip (recipe follows), for topping (optional)

1. In a large mixing bowl, sift together the flour, sugar, baking powder, baking soda, cinnamon, and salt.

2. In a small mixing bowl, whisk together the nut milk and water.

3. Slowly add the wet ingredients into the bowl containing the dry ingredients in thirds, stirring constantly. If you are using berries, fold in the berries after the mixture is thoroughly combined, creating a batter. Transfer the batter to a large, pourable container.

4. In a large skillet over medium heat, warm the oil. Ladle the batter onto the skillet in 2-inch- (5-cm-) wide drops. Cook for 3 to 4 minutes on the first side, until you see bubbles coming through the batter. Carefully flip the cakes and cook for another 2 to 3 minutes. The pancakes are done when they spring back if lightly touched. Repeat until all the batter is gone. Serve immediately topped with the Maple Whip (if using).

VARIATIONS: To make Cornmeal Pancakes, substitute blue or yellow cornmeal for ½ of the wheat flour.

To make Nutty Pancakes, substitute pecans for the berries, or make them with half pecans and half berries.

To make Chocolate Chip Pancakes, add 1 cup (180 g) of dairy-free semisweet chocolate or carob chips! Just be sure you gently fold these items into the batter at the end of the mixing process.

Maple Whip

What could possibly go better on pancakes than a combination of whipped "cream" AND maple syrup?! You won't be able to stop eating this one. It's also a great topping for holiday pies, brownies, fruit, hot drinks, or even just by itself, for a sweet treat.

YIELD: **1½ cups (356 mL)**

- **1 (12-ounce [341-g]) package silken tofu, drained**
- **¼ cup (59 mL) pure maple syrup**
- **1 tablespoon agave nectar**
- **1 tablespoon pure vanilla extract**
- **1 teaspoon grapeseed oil**

1. In a blender, combine all of the ingredients. Blend on high for 3 minutes or until fully combined.

2. Chill in the refrigerator for at least 15 minutes before serving.

Banana Berry Bran Muffins

If you're a fan of both a great bran muffin and low-fat sweets, you'll love this recipe. These muffins are loaded with bran and fresh fruit, making them a fiber-packed, yet delicious, breakfast snack.

YIELD: **1½ dozen medium-sized muffins**

- 1½ cups (203 g) whole wheat flour
- 1¼ cups (169 g) wheat bran plus more, for sprinkling
- 1 teaspoon baking powder
- 1 teaspoon baking soda
- ½ teaspoon sea salt
- 2 dashes ground cinnamon
- 3 ripe bananas (fresh or frozen)
- ¾ cup (178 mL) agave nectar
- ½ cup (119 mL) almond milk
- ¼ cup (59 mL) orange juice
- ¼ cup (59 mL) molasses
- 2 tablespoons vegetable oil
- 1½ cups (249 g) fresh or frozen and thawed berries

1. Preheat the oven to 350°F (180°C). Lightly grease 3 muffin tins.

2. In a large mixing bowl, sift together the flour, bran, baking powder, baking soda, salt, and cinnamon.

3. Place the bananas in another large mixing bowl and mash them thoroughly. (If the bananas are frozen, thaw them and keep the liquid before mashing.) Add the agave nectar, almond milk, orange juice, molasses, and oil and mix well.

4. Pour the banana mixture into the bran and flour mixture. Stir until the batter is just moistened throughout.

5. Fold the berries into the batter.

6. Spoon the batter into the prepared muffin tins and bake for 15 to 20 minutes. Remove from the oven. Let cool on a wire rack for 15 minutes and remove from the tins. Serve.

BAKERS' NOTE: Lightly toasting nuts or seeds before baking with them really enhances their flavor. Also, wet batters can make nuts too soft if they're not toasted. To toast nuts or seeds, heat a small dry skillet over medium–low heat and carefully toast the nuts in the skillet until they become fragrant. You really have to watch this, because nuts burn easily. Remove from the heat as soon as the fragrance is released.

VARIATIONS: You can use dried fruit, such as raisins or currants, in place of the fresh fruit. To make Nutty Muffins, add ⅔ cup (66 g) toasted walnuts to the batter.

Apple Streusel Coffee Cake

Coffee cakes often call to mind holiday or Sunday-brunch feasts. They really are a wonderful treat to have on special occasions or to take to a friend as a token of goodwill. Try using locally abundant fruit, as we've done here with apples.

YIELD: **1 (8-inch) coffee cake**

For the Filling:

- 1 cup (100 g) pecan halves
- 1 tablespoon vegetable oil
- 2 medium tart apples, peeled, cored, and diced

For the Streusel:

- 1 cup (135 g) whole wheat pastry flour
- ½ cup (100 g) organic granulated cane sugar
- ⅓ cup (70 g) vegan margarine (Earth Balance), softened, at room temperature
- 1 teaspoon ground cinnamon
- ½ teaspoon baking powder
- Pinch sea salt

For the Cake:

- 1 cup (135 g) whole wheat flour
- 1 cup (106 g) unbleached organic pastry flour
- 2 teaspoons baking powder
- 2 teaspoons baking soda
- 1 teaspoon ground cinnamon
- 1 teaspoon ground ginger
- ½ teaspoon ground nutmeg
- ½ teaspoon dry ground mustard
- ½ teaspoon ground cloves
- ¾ cup (178 mL) pure maple syrup
- ¾ cup (178 mL) water
- ⅓ cup (79 mL) vegetable oil
- 1 tablespoon apple cider vinegar
- 1 tablespoon pure vanilla extract
- ½ teaspoon sea salt

To make the Filling:

1. Preheat the oven to 350°F (180°C).

2. Place the pecan halves on a dry baking sheet. Toast the pecans in the oven for 12 minutes. Remove from the oven. Let them cool, and then coarsely chop them.

3. In a large sauté pan over medium–high heat, warm the oil. Add the apples and stir continuously for 3 minutes, until they start to soften. Remove from the heat.

4. In a large mixing bowl, thoroughly combine the apples and toasted pecans. Set aside.

To make the Streusel:

1. In a large mixing bowl, combine the pastry flour, sugar, margarine, cinnamon, baking powder, and salt. Using your clean fingers, toss the mixture together until it is moistened and clumpy. You are done tossing when the mixture has the consistency of wet, pebbly sand. Add a few drops of water if necessary. Set aside.

To make the Cake:

1. Lightly grease an 8-inch (20-cm) springform pan.

2. In a large mixing bowl, sift together the flours, baking powder, baking soda, salt, and spices. Set aside.

3. In a medium mixing bowl, whisk together the maple syrup, water, oil, vinegar, and vanilla extract, until the mixture is thoroughly blended.

4. Pour the wet ingredients into the bowl containing the dry ingredients. Whisk the mixtures together until the liquid is completely absorbed. (Be sure to scrape the sides of the bowl to make sure all the dry ingredients are mixed in.) Don't worry if a few small lumps remain—they will disappear when baked.

5. Cover the bottom of the prepared springform pan with 2 cups (474 mL) of the batter. Next, pour the Filling into the springform pan on top of the batter, taking care to evenly distribute it.

6. Pour the remaining cake batter on top of the Filling, covering it completely. Sprinkle the Streusel evenly on top of the batter.

7. Bake for 1 hour. Remove from the oven. Allow the cake to cool in the pan on a wire rack for 30 minutes before releasing it from the pan, cutting it, and serving it.

BAKERS' NOTE: If you don't happen to have whole wheat flour, you can always substitute unbleached organic all-purpose flour.

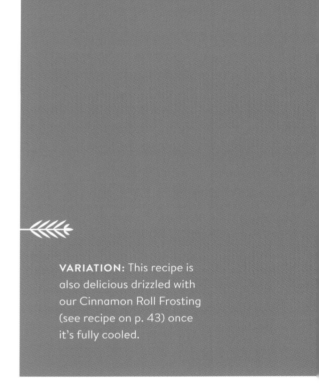

VARIATION: This recipe is also delicious drizzled with our Cinnamon Roll Frosting (see recipe on p. 43) once it's fully cooled.

French Toast with Blueberry Compote

You may have feared you'd have to give up deliciously decadent treats like French toast after taking the vegan plunge. Not so! This eggless French toast does not disappoint.

YIELD: **12 pieces French toast (1 loaf)**

- 24 ounces (720 mL) coconut milk
- ¼ cup (59 mL) canola oil
- ¼ cup (59 mL) organic granulated cane sugar
- 1 tablespoon egg replacer
- 1 tablespoon pure vanilla extract
- 1½ teaspoons ground cinnamon
- 1½ teaspoons ground turmeric
- 1 loaf quality bread
- 2 teaspoons canola oil, for frying

1. In a large mixing bowl, combine all of the ingredients except the bread and oil. Blend the ingredients together with a hand mixer on medium speed for 3 to 5 minutes, until a batter forms.

2. Pour the batter into a greased 9 × 12-inch (22.5 × 30-cm) baking dish. Dip each slice of bread in the batter until it is fully coated.

3. In a large nonstick skillet over medium-high heat, warm the oil. Cook each slice for 2 to 3 minutes per side, until golden brown. As you cook each slice, transfer it to a serving platter covered with foil. Serve immediately.

Blueberry Compote

Blueberries are huge during Midwestern summers, so this is a good recipe for locavores in the area. If blueberries aren't plentiful in your area, make this recipe with a different locally available seasonal berry instead.

YIELD: **2 cups (474 mL)**

- 2⅔ cups (386 g) blueberries
- ¼ cup (50 g) organic granulated cane sugar
- 1½ tablespoons fresh lemon juice
- 1 teaspoon cornstarch
- 2 tablespoons cold water

1. In a small saucepan over medium heat, combine the blueberries, sugar, and lemon juice. Bring to a boil. Remove from the heat and set aside.

2. In a small mixing bowl, whisk together the cornstarch and water.

3. Add the cornstarch and water slurry to the saucepan. Return the saucepan to medium heat. Bring to a boil. Remove from the heat.

4. Allow the compote to stand for 3 to 5 minutes. Serve warm over French toast or pancakes.

VARIATION: If you're avoiding corn products or just happen to have arrowroot powder in your pantry, feel free to substitute it for the cornstarch. 

Biscuits and White Sage Gravy

When you decide to go veg and eat more consciously, it doesn't mean you don't still crave the hearty, down-home breakfasts of your youth. Our Biscuits and White Sage Gravy will take you there! The biscuits are great on their own with a little vegan margarine or some apple butter. The gravy can be used to top just about anything, including mashed potatoes!

YIELD: **10–12 biscuits**

- Cooking spray, for greasing
- 2½–3 cups (593–711 mL) soy or almond milk
- 1 tablespoon apple cider vinegar
- 5 cups (605 g) unbleached organic all-purpose flour
- 1½ tablespoons baking powder
- 1 teaspoon baking soda
- 1 teaspoon fresh chives
- ½ teaspoon sea salt
- 1 clove garlic, minced
- ¼ teaspoon freshly ground black pepper
- ⅛ teaspoon dried rosemary
- 1½ sticks vegan margarine, very cold and cut into cubes
- 1 tablespoon melted vegan margarine, for brushing
- White Sage Gravy (recipe follows), for serving

1. Preheat the oven to 325°F (160°C). Lightly grease a baking sheet with the cooking spray and set aside.

2. In a medium mixing bowl, whisk together the soy milk and vinegar, making a vegan buttermilk. Set aside.

3. In a large mixing bowl, sift together the flour, baking powder, and baking soda. Add the chives, salt, garlic, black pepper, and rosemary. Mix well.

4. Using a fork or pastry blender, cut the margarine into the flour mixture until it resembles coarse cornmeal.

5. Add the vegan buttermilk to the large mixing bowl. Mix gently until just combined, forming a dough.

6. When the dough comes together, take it out of the bowl. The dough should be smooth and elastic. On a lightly floured work surface, roll out the dough to a ¾-inch (1.9-cm) thickness. Cut out biscuit rounds with a biscuit cutter or a glass. As you cut out each biscuit round, place it on the prepared baking sheet. When you no longer have room in the dough to cut another biscuit round, gently recombine the dough, roll it out again, and cut out more biscuit rounds. Roll out the dough no more than three times, or your dough will become too sticky and overworked.

7. Brush each biscuit round with the melted margarine. Bake for 15 to 20 minutes, until the tops of the biscuits are golden brown and a cake tester inserted in the middle of 1 of the biscuits comes out clean. Remove from the oven. Serve warm immediately with the White Sage Gravy.

BAKERS' NOTE: "Cutting in" is a baking term used to describe the addition of a solid fat to a flour or dry mixture.

VARIATIONS: For Traditional Biscuits, omit the herbs from the recipe and add 2 tablespoons of fresh lemon juice in their place.

For a biscuit that contains less gluten, use only 2½ cups (303 g) of unbleached organic all-purpose flour and substitute cornmeal or buckwheat flour for the remaining 2½ cups (303 g) of flour.

White Sage Gravy

Gravy is one of those versatile sauces that makes just about everything a little more delicious.

YIELD: **4 cups (948 mL)**

- **1 cup (224 g) vegan margarine (like Earth Balance)**
- **2 cups (300 g) minced onion**
- **1 cup (158 g) rice flour**
- **2 tablespoons vegetable bouillon dissolved in ¼ cup soy milk**
- **8 cups (1.9 L) water or vegetable stock**
- **2 tablespoons onion powder**
- **2 tablespoons fresh chopped or 1 teaspoon dried sage**
- **1 tablespoon dried marjoram**
- **1 tablespoon nutritional yeast flakes**
- **1 teaspoon white pepper**
- **Sea salt and freshly ground black pepper, to taste**

1. In a large saucepan over medium heat, melt the margarine. Add the onion and sauté until it is caramelized.

2. Slowly sift the flour into the saucepan, whisking constantly until it is completely blended. Cook for 5 minutes, stirring constantly, until a golden brown roux forms.

3. Slowly add the vegetable stock and water to the saucepan, still whisking constantly.

4. Add all of the remaining ingredients to the saucepan. Raise the heat to medium-high and bring to a boil. Lower the heat to low and simmer the gravy for 8 minutes, until the desired thickness is reached. Remove from the heat and transfer to a gravy boat.

COOKS' NOTE: You can easily thicken up a too-thin gravy by slowly adding 1 tablespoon of flour or nutritional yeast flakes, but be sure to whisk vigorously and constantly while adding it to avoid lumps.

VARIATION: Want to give your gravy a little more substance? Try tossing 1½ cups (85 g) of Breakfast Chorizo (see recipe on p. 28) into the gravy just before it is finished cooking.

Chai Spice Scones with Maple Glaze

There's something about this sweet breakfast biscuit that really sets it apart from all other breakfast pastries and breads. Maybe it's the scone's dense drop-biscuit texture, dried fruits, and spices that combine to make it crumble so perfectly into a morning coffee or tea cup. These scones are topped with a sweet Maple Glaze that goes well on any breakfast bread, muffin, or cookie.

YIELD: **1 dozen scones;**
1 cup (237 mL) Maple Glaze

For the Maple Glaze:

- ½ **cup (50g) organic confectioners' sugar**
- 3 **tablespoons (45 mL) pure maple syrup**
- ½–1 **tablespoon soy milk, plus more if needed**

For the Scones:

- 3¾ **cups (399 g) whole wheat pastry flour**
- 2½ **cups (303 g) unbleached organic all-purpose flour**
- 3 **teaspoons baking powder**
- 2½ **teaspoons ground cinnamon**
- 2¼ **teaspoons ground cardamom**
- 2 **teaspoons sea salt**
- 1¼ **teaspoons ground ginger**
- ¾ **teaspoon ground cloves**
- ¼ **teaspoon white pepper**
- 1 **cup (200 g) organic granulated cane sugar**
- 1⅔ **cups (395 mL) soy milk, plus more if needed**
- 1 **cup (224 g) vegan margarine (Earth Balance), chilled**
- 1 **tablespoon pure vanilla extract**

To make the Maple Glaze:

1. In a small mixing bowl, whisk together all of the ingredients. The mixture should be very smooth and runny, as it will be poured on the scones. Add more soy milk, if needed, by the teaspoon until the desired consistency is reached. Set aside at room temperature.

To make the Scones:

1. Preheat the oven to 350°F (180°C). Line a baking sheet with parchment paper. Set aside.

2. In a large mixing bowl, sift together the flours, baking powder, sugar, cinnamon, cardamom, salt, ginger, cloves, and white pepper.

3. Cut in the margarine just as you would when making biscuits (see recipes on pp. 40 and 161). Set aside.

4. In a small mixing bowl, whisk together the soy milk, and vanilla extract. Gradually add the wet mixture to the dry mixture until just combined. Stir well. (Be sure to scrape the sides of the bowl to make sure all the dry ingredients are thoroughly mixed.) If the mixture is too dry, add more soy milk, 1 tablespoon at a time, until the dough holds together. Be sure not to overwork the dough.

5. Using an ice cream scoop, make ½-cup (119-mL) dollops of dough. Place each dollop on the prepared baking sheet, about 2 inches (5 cm) apart.

6. Bake for 20 minutes, until golden at the edges and a cake tester inserted in the center of 1 of the scones comes out clean. Remove from the oven and cool on a wire rack.

7. Once the scones have cooled, drizzle with the Maple Glaze and let it harden a bit before serving. Serve or store in an airtight container at room temperature for 3 days.

BAKERS' NOTE: You can also substitute coconut oil, grapeseed, or canola oil in most baking recipes that call for melted vegan margarine. Sometimes you want the salty, buttery flavor of margarine, but in the case of cookies and scones, coconut oil works really well.

Cinnamon Rolls

These cinnamon rolls are big and gooey, just like a good cinnamon roll should be. They're sure to be as big of a hit in your dining room as they are in ours.

YIELD: **12 rolls**

For the Dough:

- 1 tablespoon dry yeast
- ¾ cup (150 g) + ¼ teaspoon organic granulated cane sugar, divided
- ½ cup (119 mL) warm water
- 2 cups (242 g) unbleached organic all-purpose flour
- 2 cups (274 g) bread flour (or more all-purpose flour)
- ½ teaspoon sea salt
- ¼ cup (56 g) melted and cooled vegan margarine
- ¾ cup (178 mL) + 2 tablespoons soy or almond milk, divided
- Cooking spray, for greasing

For the Filling:

- ¾ cup (169 g) organic light brown sugar
- 2 tablespoons melted vegan margarine
- ½ tablespoon unbleached organic all-purpose flour
- 2 teaspoons ground cinnamon
- ½ teaspoon sea salt

For the Frosting:

- 1½ cups (150 g) organic confectioners' cane sugar
- ¼ cup (56 g) vegan margarine
- ¼ cup (56 g) vegan cream cheese (we like Tofutti)

For the Rolls:

- Cooking spray, for greasing
- 2–4 tablespoons melted and cooled vegan margarine

Continued on pg. 44

VARIATIONS: To make Chocolate Chip Scones, omit the cinnamon, cardamom, ginger, cloves, and white pepper. Instead, add 1 cup (180 g) dairy-free semisweet chocolate or carob chips.

You could also make Dried Cranberry or Cherry Scones by adding 1 cup (112 g) of dried fruit and 2 teaspoons lemon or orange zest.

Cinnamon Rolls *(Continued from pg. 43)*

To make the Dough:

1. In a small mixing bowl, whisk together the yeast, the ¼ teaspoon sugar, and the water. Cover with plastic wrap and set aside in a warm place until it begins to bubble (5 to 10 minutes depending on the room's temperature), to activate yeast.

2. In the bowl of a stand mixer fitted with the dough hook attachment, sift together the flours, the remaining sugar, and the salt on low speed until well combined.

3. Once the yeast looks foamy, it is activated. Add it to the bowl of the stand mixer, along with the margarine and the ¾ cup (178 mL) soy milk. Knead with the dough hook attachment on low speed for 30 seconds. (If you don't have a stand mixer, knead the dough by hand on a floured surface for 10 minutes.) If the dough is dry, add some or all of the remaining soy milk 1 tablespoon at a time, until the desired consistency is reached. The dough should remain a little wet and should make a light sloshing sound when mixing.

4. Continue kneading with the dough hook on low speed for 3 minutes. Raise the speed 1 level and knead for another 3 to 6 minutes, until the dough pulls away from the bowl. The dough is ready when you can stretch it very thinly without breaking it.

5. Lightly grease a large mixing bowl with the cooking spray. Transfer the dough to the mixing bowl and cover with plastic wrap. Keep in a warm place for 2 hours, until it doubles in size.

To make the Filling:

1. In a large mixing bowl, combine all of the ingredients and whisk to mix together thoroughly. Set aside, covered, until ready to use.

To make the Frosting:

1. In a medium mixing bowl, sift the sugar. Set aside.

2. In the clean bowl of a stand mixer fitted with the paddle attachment, cream the margarine on medium-low speed for 3 minutes, until it is smooth. (Be sure to scrape the sides of the bowl several times during the creaming process.)

3. With the mixer operating at low speed, add the sugar in ¼-cup (50-g) increments. Once all the sugar has been added, increase the mixer speed to high and, using the whisk attachment, whip until fluffy. Add the cream cheese and mix on low speed until just combined. Cover the bowl and store in the refrigerator until ready to use.

To assemble the Rolls:

1. Lightly grease a 9 × 13-inch (22.5 × 32.5-cm) casserole dish or cake pan with the cooking spray.

2. On a floured surface, roll out the proofed dough until you form a 7½ × 10-inch (19 × 25-cm) rectangle.

3. Coat the dough rectangle evenly with the Filling, leaving an inch bare at one of the rectangle's long ends.

4. Roll the rectangle into a cylindrical shape tightly onto itself, with the bare end rolling up last. Press the bare end firmly to seal it. Brush the dough cylinder with the margarine and cut into 12 1½–2-inch- (4–5-cm-) thick slices.

5. Transfer the rolls to the prepared baking dish. Cover with plastic wrap. Keep in a warm place for 2 hours, until the rolls double in size.

6. Preheat the oven to 350°F (180°C).

7. Bake for 12 to 15 minutes, until golden brown. Remove from the oven and place on a wire rack to cool.

8. Spread the rolls with the Frosting while they are still slightly warm. Serve or store in an airtight container at room temperature for 3 to 4 days.

Green Smoothie

It's no accident that the smoothie craze has really taken off. These breakfast drinks are extremely refreshing, hydrating, and energizing. While all smoothies are a great kick-start in the morning, there's something instantly invigorating about the green ones—especially when you've overimbibed the night before. It's like a hangover-curing hydration charge in a glass. Start drinking these every morning, and chances are, you'll notice that your skin will begin to glow and your energy levels will start to soar within days.

YIELD: **4 (8-ounce [240-mL]) smoothies**

- **3 stalks organic celery**
- **1 red pear, quartered**
- **1 banana, halved**
- **1 orange, quartered**
- **1 cup (65 g) kale**
- **1 cup (36 g) organic romaine lettuce**
- **½ cup (8 g) chopped cilantro**
- **Juice of 1 orange (or lemon)**
- **Purified water, to fill**

1. Place all of the ingredients in a blender. Fill the blender halfway with the purified water and purée until the mixture is smooth and liquefied. Pour the smoothies into tall glasses and serve immediately.

COOKS' NOTES: Banana or avocado in a smoothie gives the drink a smooth consistency.

Don't forget to give your blender a break: Cut your fruit into 1-inch (2.5-cm) pieces for blending ease.

Greens should be torn, not cut.

You can substitute any green, such as spinach or chard, for the kale. The same goes for the cilantro—use fresh parsley instead you are averse to cilantro.

Experiment as you get used to drinking green smoothies, changing out the fruits and greens but keeping the proportions comparable.

Try to balance sweet, yet low-glycemic, fruits (such as strawberries, apples, peaches, oranges, and cherries) with greens so your drink stays tasty but is also packed with nutrients.

TIME SAVER: Store any leftover smoothie in a tightly sealed Mason jar or Nalgene bottle for a healthy breakfast on the go.

Local Fruit Smoothie

Fruit smoothies are delicious, and that's really all there is to it. Eating fruit in the morning is a great way to get your metabolism going while reaping the bounty of your area's best local fruits.

YIELD: **4 (8-ounce [240-mL]) smoothies**

- **3 cups (498 g) frozen local berries**
- **2½ cups (593 mL) unsweetened almond milk, or just enough to just cover the berries**
- **3 tablespoons (45 mL) agave nectar or pure maple syrup**
- **2 tablespoons milled flaxseed or whole chia seeds**

1. Place all the fruit in a blender.

2. Cover the fruit with the almond milk.

3. Add the remaining ingredients and blend on low for 90 seconds. Stir well. Blend on high for another 2 to 3 minutes, until the mixture is smooth and liquefied. Pour the smoothies into tall glasses and serve immediately.

COOKS' NOTE: If you live in a cold climate, stock up on farmstand fresh fruit in the summer and freeze it so you can enjoy your smoothies all winter long.

Entertaining

Hosting your own gathering gives you a great opportunity to showcase some of the incredible creativity and flavor involved in vegan cooking. Mickey and Jo started the Diner so they'd always have a place to eat. Think of entertaining in your home the same way! Pair our signature cocktails with the scrumptious veggie apps you'll find on the pages that follow. Your friends and family will surely raise a glass to these inventive recipes.

PICTURED: **"Meatballs" with BBQ Sauce (p. 50)**

Sweet Potato Quesadilla

Mexican-inspired dishes are always a hit at the Diner. For this creation, we used ingredients we already had in the kitchen to come up with a new recipe. It's a simply delicious dish that's great for adults and kids alike. This nutrient-packed twist on a fan favorite is especially great served with our Mezcal Mule (recipe follows); the combination of sweet, savory, and smoky tones is sure to satisfy.

YIELD: **4 quesadilla wedges**

- **1 tablespoon vegetable oil**
- **1 8-inch (20-cm) whole-grain tortilla**
- **⅓ cup (70 g) cooked Mashed Sweet Potatoes (see recipe on p. 143)**
- **⅓ cup (57 g) cooked Spiced Black Beans (see recipe on p. 146 or use canned vegan refried black beans)**
- **⅓ cup (76 g) Chorizo Seitan (see recipe on p. 28 or try the Trader Joe's brand)**
- **⅓ cup (37 g) vegan mozzarella-style cheese (try Trader Joe's vegan mozzarella shreds)**
- **1 handful baby spinach, chopped**
- **Sliced avocado, vegan sour cream, and sliced scallions, for garnish (optional)**

1. Warm a nonstick or electric skillet over medium heat. Once the skillet is warm, add the oil.

2. On a clean work surface, place the tortilla. Spread the sweet potatoes, beans, seitan, vegan cheese, and spinach onto half the tortilla.

3. Fold the tortilla in half and place it in the skillet. Use a spatula to press the quesadilla down flat. Move it around the skillet a bit as it cooks. After 5 minutes, or as it starts to turn golden, carefully flip the quesadilla over. Gently pat it with the spatula to flatten it out. (This is especially useful for getting the vegan cheese to spread out and melt evenly.) Lightly move the quesadilla around in the skillet to keep it from sticking.

4. Continue moving and gently patting the quesadilla until both sides are golden brown. Remove from the heat and place on a cutting surface.

5. Cut the quesadilla into 4 wedges. Serve topped with the avocado, vegan sour cream, and scallions, if desired.

VARIATION: Try using Hickory Tempeh Crumbles (see recipe on p. 21) or Seitan Bacun Strips (see recipe on p. 23) instead of the Chorizo Seitan. You can also add slices of fresh hot peppers, either as a topping or inside the quesadilla.

Mezcal Mule

Mezcal is a wonderful spirit that begs to be paired with food, but it can stand on its own in this fantastic and simple cocktail. Here, the heavy campfire smoke of a craft mezcal is balanced by the sweet and refreshing flavors of fresh lime and ginger beer.

YIELD: **1 cocktail**

- **1½ ounces (45 mL) mezcal (we use the El Malpais brand)**
- **3 ounces (90 mL) ginger beer**
- **Juice of ½ lime**
- **Lime wheel, for garnish**

1. Build all of the ingredients except the lime wheel into an iced rocks glass and garnish with a lime wheel.

IMBIBERS' NOTE: Some versions of this recipe include garnishes like cucumber, chiles, and passionfruit. Be creative and dress up the Mule however you like!

"Meatballs" with BBQ Sauce

Amp up your BBQs and Super Bowl parties Chicago-Diner-style with seitan "meatballs" and spiked Logan Square Lemonade (recipe follows).

YIELD: **16 "meatballs" and 2 cups (474 mL) sauce**

For the Meatballs:

- **Cooking spray, for greasing**
- **8 cups (227 g) ground seitan (make your own using the recipe on p. 22 or buy from your local grocery store)**
- **2 cups (300 g) chopped onions**
- **2 cups (300 g) panko or other vegan bread crumbs**
- **½ cup (119 mL) ketchup**
- **¼ cup (59 mL) A-1 sauce**
- **2 tablespoons vegetable bouillon**
- **3 teaspoons dried basil**
- **3 teaspoons dried oregano**
- **1½ teaspoons granulated garlic**
- **1 teaspoon sea salt**

For the BBQ Sauce:

- **1 tablespoon grapeseed oil**
- **½ cup (75 g) minced onion**
- **½ cup (110 g) tomato puree**
- **½ cup (80 g) diced tomatoes**
- **¼ cup (59 mL) apple cider vinegar**
- **¼ cup (59 mL) molasses**
- **3½ tablespoons (49 g) organic light brown sugar**
- **2 tablespoons orange juice**
- **1 tablespoon tomato paste**
- **1 teaspoon sea salt**
- **¾ teaspoon chili powder**
- **¾ teaspoon granulated garlic**
- **¾ teaspoon ground plain paprika**
- **¾ teaspoon freshly ground black pepper**
- **½ tablespoon Dijon-style mustard**
- **½ teaspoon liquid smoke**
- **½ teaspoon onion powder**
- **Dash ground cumin**
- **Dash dry ground mustard**

To make the Meatballs:

1. Preheat the oven to 350°F (180°C). Lightly grease a baking sheet with the cooking spray.

2. In a large mixing bowl, mix together all of the ingredients with your clean hands. Roll the mixture into 16 1- to 1½-inch (2.5–4-cm) meatballs.

3. Place the "meatballs" on the prepared baking sheet. Bake for 15 minutes. Remove from the oven and set aside to cool slightly.

To make the BBQ Sauce:

1. In a medium saucepan over medium heat, warm the oil. Add the onion and sauté it until it becomes translucent.

2. Add the remaining ingredients. Reduce the heat and simmer for 10 to 15 minutes. Remove from the heat.

3. With an immersion blender, purée the sauce. (If you do not have an immersion blender, allow the sauce to cool slightly and transfer it to a food processor fitted with the metal "S" blade or a blender for puréeing. If you must transfer the sauce, return the sauce to the saucepan before proceeding to the next step.)

4. Add the "meatballs" and mix them with the sauce until they are fully covered. Keep the "meatballs" and sauce warm in a crockpot or stockpot over low heat until they are ready to serve. (It's a good idea to have toothpicks on hand so guests can enjoy them with ease.) Serve.

Logan Square Lemonade

A summer outing or sporting event is the perfect time to serve America's oldest whiskey. Rye came to be during the Revolutionary War, when blockades prevented the colonists from getting rum from the Caribbean islands. They turned locavore and started making their own booze. Though it went out of fashion for decades, rye was the foundation of all 19th century whiskey drinks.

YIELD: **1 cocktail**

- 2 ounces (60 mL) rye whiskey
- 4 ounces (120 mL) natural lemonade
- 2 dashes bitters (we prefer the Fee Brothers brand)
- Lemon wheel, for garnish

1. In a cocktail shaker filled with ice, combine all of the ingredients except the lemon wheel and shake until well combined and very cold. Strain the cocktail into an iced rocks glass. Garnish with the lemon wheel and serve.

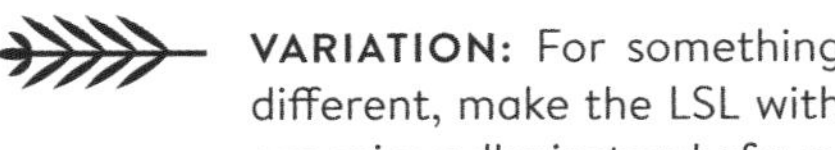

VARIATION: For something different, make the LSL with organic vodka instead of rye.

Bacun Wrapped Dates

This one's sweet and spicy. These delectable dates were a huge hit at the opening reception for the Diner location in Logan Square. Try them with our Logan Bloody Mary (recipe follows). The porter and whiskey added to our Bloody add a hearty, smoky flavor reminiscent of vegan bacun. As the drink's creator remarked, "what argument do you need to put whiskey and [vegan] bacun together?"

YIELD: **12 dates**

- 12 dates
- 3–6 jalapeño peppers, seeded and sliced
- 12 strips vegan bacun (make your own [see recipe on p. 23] or try the Lightlife brand)
- Toothpicks, for serving
- Canola oil, for pan frying

1. Pit the dates and place a sliver of pepper in place of each date's pit.

2. Wrap each date with a slice of bacun and secure with a toothpick.

3. Into a deep skillet, pour 2 inches (5 cm) of the oil. Heat the oil over medium heat. When the oil begins to bubble, add the dates. Moving the dates around constantly to ensure even cooking, pan fry them until the bacun is crisp on all sides. Remove from the heat and serve.

Logan Bloody Mary

YIELD: **4 cups (948 mL) Bloody Mary Mix; 1 Bloody Mary cocktail**

For the Bloody Mary Mix:

- 1 (30-ounce [900-mL]) bottle tomato juice
- 1 ounce (30 mL) fresh lemon juice
- 1 tablespoon organic granulated cane sugar
- ½ tablespoon (heaping) freshly ground black pepper
- ½ tablespoon grated horseradish
- ½ teaspoon celery salt, or to taste
- 2 heavy dashes Sriracha or other hot sauce, or to taste

For the Cocktail:

- 1½ ounces (45 mL) white whiskey or vodka
- 3–4 ounces (90–120 mL) Bloody Mary Mix
- 1 ounce (30 mL) porter beer (try Great Lakes Edmund Fitzgerald)
- 2 dashes celery bitters (try Fee Brothers)
- Freshly ground black pepper, to taste
- Celery, green olive, and dill pickle, for garnish

To make the Bloody Mary Mix:

1. In a large pitcher, combine all of the ingredients except the celery salt and hot sauce and stir with a whisk. Add the celery salt and Sriracha sauce, adjusting to taste. Use immediately or store in an airtight container in the refrigerator for up to 1 week.

To make the Cocktail:

1. In a pint glass filled halfway with ice, combine the whiskey or vodka, the Bloody Mary Mix, and the porter. Stir well. Add the bitters. Top with the black pepper. Garnish with the celery, olive, and pickle.

TIME SAVER: Having Bloody Mary mix around is useful! It's the perfect kickstarter for your day if you had a few too many Logan Square Lemonades (see recipe on p. 51) the night before.

Ginger Coconut Tofu Bites

These are tasty, easy-to-make, and elegant party hors d'oeuvres. Serve guests the bites alongside our Black Rainbow Unicorn cocktail (recipe follows). The resonating coconut and ginger flavors will knock their socks off.

YIELD: **24 bites**

- 2 (12-ounce [341-g]) blocks extra-firm tofu
- 2 cups (240 g) cornstarch
- 1 tablespoon + 1 teaspoon ground ginger
- ½ cup (119 mL) agave nectar
- 2 teaspoons dry ground mustard
- 2 teaspoons sea salt
- 1 cup (237 mL) vegetable or coconut oil, divided
- Cooking spray, for greasing
- ¼ cup (23 g) toasted coconut shreds

1. Place the tofu on a paper towel and allow it to drain at room temperature for 30 minutes. (If you're in a hurry, you can gently press out the moisture with a cheesecloth.)

2. In a medium mixing bowl, sift or whisk together the cornstarch and ginger.

3. In another small mixing bowl, whisk together the agave, mustard, and sea salt, creating a dressing.

4. Cut the tofu into ½-inch (13-mm) cubes. Toss the cubes in the cornstarch mixture until each piece is thoroughly covered.

5. In a large nonstick skillet over medium-high heat, warm about half the oil. When the oil begins to bubble, add half the tofu to the skillet. Fry the tofu bites on each side for 4 to 5 minutes, or until golden brown.

6. Add the remaining oil to the skillet if needed, and when it begins to bubble, add the remaining half of the tofu to the skillet. Fry on each side for 4 to 5 minutes, or until golden brown. Remove from the heat.

7. Allow the bites to cool completely on a paper towel. After they have cooled, place them in the mixing bowl containing the agave mustard dressing and toss until thoroughly coated. You will likely have to do this in batches.

8. Preheat the oven to 325°F (160°C). Lightly grease a baking sheet with the cooking spray.

9. Toss the bites in the shredded coconut until evenly coated, and then transfer to the prepared baking sheet.

10. Bake the bites for 7 to 10 minutes. Remove from the oven and transfer to a platter. Serve immediately.

COOKS' NOTE: If you don't have coconut in your pantry, you can substitute toasted hemp seeds for a nuttier flavor. To toast the seeds, bake them at 275°F (140°) for 10 minutes, stirring them at least once during the baking time.

Black Rainbow Unicorn with Grenadine and House Cherries

The name lures you in, and the luscious hibiscus and spice flavors keep you coming back for more. Hum is a botanical spirit infused with hibiscus, ginger root, cardamom, and kaffir lime. Coconut milk and house-made Grenadine are the perfect accompaniments for this delicious spirit.

YIELD: 16 ounces (480 mL) Grenadine syrup; 12 ounces (341 g) House Cherries; 1 cocktail

---

For the Grenadine and House Cherries:

- 2 cups (474 mL) pomegranate juice (fresh is best)
- ¾ cup (150 g) organic granulated cane sugar
- Juice of 1 lemon wedge
- ½ teaspoon orange zest
- 10–12 ounces (284–341 g) frozen dark cherries

For the Cocktail:

- 1 ounce (30 mL) hum
- 2 ounces (60 mL) orange juice
- 1 ounce (30 mL) coconut milk
- Dash Grenadine
- House Cherry, for garnish

To make the Grenadine and House Cherries:

1. In a large saucepan over medium heat, warm all of the ingredients except the cherries. Bring to a gentle simmer until the mixture reduces to a syrupy thickness. (Be careful to never allow it to reach a full boil.)

2. Transfer to an open jar and allow to cool to room temperature.

3. Gently stir in the frozen cherries. Cover and refrigerate overnight.

4. Stir again before removing the cherries from the syrup. Remove the cherries with a slotted spoon or by gently pouring the mixture through a mesh strainer and reserving the syrup. Carefully pour the syrup and the cherries into separate airtight bottles and store for up to 2 weeks in the refrigerator.

To make the Cocktail:

1. In a cocktail shaker filled with ice, combine all of the ingredients except the House Cherry and shake until well combined and very cold. Strain the cocktail into an iced rocks glass or martini glass. Garnish with the House Cherry and serve.

NOTE: If you're not up for making your own grenadine and cherries, you can use storebought versions of either. However, if you are sticking to a vegan diet, be aware that most refined cane sugar in the United States is not vegan. It is filtered and whitened using bone char from cows. Often, products made using sugar do not indicate what kind of sugar is used. Beet sugar and organic sugar are vegan. We use Florida Crystals brand evaporated cane juice, which is vegan. High-fructose corn syrup (HFCS) may be vegan, but we don't recommend buying products containing this sweetener.

Savory Tomato Tartlettes

These delightful tarts are perfect for events with standing room only since there's no utensils needed. Try serving these with our wonderful Ghost of the Congress cocktail (recipe follows) because, well, as our bar manager says, "When in doubt, serve whiskey."

YIELD: **2 dozen tartlettes**

For the Crust:

- 2½ cups (303 g) unbleached organic all-purpose flour
- 1 teaspoon sea salt
- 1 cup (224 g) vegan margarine, very cold and cut into small cubes
- ¼–½ cup (59–119 mL) ice water
- Cooking spray, for greasing

For the Filling:

- 2½ pounds (1.13 kg) medium tomatoes, cored and roughly chopped
- 1 medium onion, thinly sliced
- ¼ cup (59 mL) extra virgin olive oil
- Freshly ground black pepper, to taste
- ¾ cup (170 g) Tofu Ricotta (see recipe on p. 25)
- ½ cup (67 g) pitted kalamata olives
- ¼ cup (30 g) capers
- Fresh thyme, to taste

Continued on pg. 58

Savory Tomato Tartlettes *(Continued from pg. 57)*

To make the Crust:

1. In the bowl of a food processor fitted with the metal "S" blade, pulse the flour and salt together. Add the margarine and pulse until the mixture takes on a coarse, pebble-like consistency (10 seconds).

2. Continue to pulse the food processor while adding ¼ cup (59 mL) ice water in a slow and steady stream. Add more water, 1 tablespoon at a time, as needed until dough just comes together. Remove the dough from the processor and place in a covered bowl. Refrigerate for 1 hour or so. You can refrigerate a little longer, but it will dry out.

3. Lightly grease 2 mini muffin pans with the cooking spray. Roll the dough into 24 small balls. Drop each ball into a muffin cup. Press the dough evenly into the sides of the muffin cups, shaping a crust. Go around the edges of each tartlette with a fork to create an attractive border.

To Make the Filling:

1. Preheat the oven to 400°F (200°C). Line a baking sheet with parchment paper.

2. In a medium mixing bowl, place the tomatoes and onions. Drizzle on the oil and then season with the black pepper. Mix well.

3. Place the tomato and onion mixture on the prepared baking sheet. Bake for 30 minutes, until the tomatoes start to shrivel and the onions are browned. Remove from the oven and transfer to a bowl. Set aside and allow to cool. Reduce the oven temperature to 375°F (190°C). When the tomatoes and onions have cooled completely, chop them up. Return to the bowl and set aside.

4. Place the Tofu Ricotta in the bowl of a food processor fitted with the metal "S" blade and pulse a few times. Toss the Tofu Ricotta with the olives, capers, and thyme. Mix well.

5. Using only half of the Tofu Ricotta mixture, fill each dough pocket in the muffin pans. Top each pocket with a portion of the tomato and onion mixture. Using the remaining half of the Tofu Ricotta mixture, sprinkle some of the mixture over the top of each pocket.

6. Bake for 45 to 60 minutes, until the top of each crust is golden brown and the filling is bubbling. Remove from the oven and cool in the muffin pans on wire racks. Remove the tartlettes from the pans, transfer to a platter, and serve.

COOKS' NOTE: In step 4 of this recipe, a food processor is used to make the Tofu Ricotta. Doing so creates a finer texture, which works better on the small tartlettes. You can skip this blending part if you don't have a food processor.

Ghost of the Congress

YIELD: **1 cocktail**

- **1½ ounces (45 mL) white whiskey (we like Journeyman Distillery's W.R. White Whiskey)**
- **1 ounce (30 mL) triple sec (Bols, vegan)**
- **½ ounce (15 mL) organic simple syrup**
- **Dash rhubarb bitters**
- **House Cherry (see recipe on p. 59), for garnish**

1. In a cocktail shaker filled with ice, combine all of the ingredients except the House Cherry and shake until well combined and very cold. Strain the cocktail into an iced rocks glass or martini glass. Garnish with the House Cherry and serve.

Crostini with Olive Tapenade

Crostini are a simple and impressive way to make crowd-pleasing appetizers in minutes. You can top them with just about anything, toss them in a salad, or use them as dipping crackers. Here we pair them with Olive Tapenade, but you could also spread them with hummus, pesto, artichoke spread, or caponata. The tapenade also has a variety of uses. You can spread it on bruschetta, sandwiches, or even pizza. Round out the heavy flavors in this dish with the aromatic components in our popular Dillinger cocktail (see recipe on p. 61).

YIELD: **12 Crostini and 1½ cups (201 g) Tapenade**

For the Crostini:

- **1 fresh long bread loaf, such as a baguette**
- **⅓ cup (79 mL) extra virgin olive oil, for brushing**
- **2 cloves garlic, minced**

For the Tapenade:

- **½ cup (67 g) pitted kalamata olives**
- **½ cup (67 g) green olives with pimentos (or add ¼ cup pimentos)**
- **2 tablespoons capers**
- **2 tablespoons extra virgin olive oil**
- **2 tablespoons sundried tomatoes**
- **2 cloves garlic**
- **½ teaspoon dried oregano**
- **½ teaspoon dried basil**
- **Chopped fresh basil, parsley, or chives, for sprinkling (optional)**

To make the Crostini:

1. Preheat the oven to 325°F (160°C). Slice the loaf of bread into 12 1- to 2-inch-thick Crostini slices and place the slices in rows on a baking sheet.

2. In a small bowl, whisk together the oil and garlic. Brush each Crostini slice with the oil mixture.

3. Bake the Crostini for 3 to 4 minutes, until the Crostini are toasted golden brown. (Be careful, as the bread burns easily.)

To make the Tapenade:

1. Carefully check each olive to ensure that all pits are removed.

2. Place all of the ingredients except the fresh herbs in the bowl of a food processor fitted with the metal "S" blade and pulse until the mixture is a smooth, yet slightly chunky, spread. Some olive chunks should remain.

3. Spread the Tapenade on the Crostini. Sprinkle with the fresh herbs, if using, and serve.

The Dillinger

Hibiscus-infused spirit plus America's first homemade liquor? Yes, please! The Dillinger is a modern spin on a classic Manhattan cocktail. Start with a good, strong rye whiskey. The thick sweetness of the Hum demands dry vermouth as a counterpart, and round it out with a dash of aromatic bitters and a House Cherry.

YIELD: **1 cocktail**

- 2 ounces (60 mL) rye whiskey (we like Journeyman Distillery's Ravenswood Rye)
- 1 ounce (30 mL) dry vermouth
- ½ ounce (15 mL) Hum (a botanical spirit; see p. 56 for details)
- Dash bitters (we prefer Fee Brothers Aromatic)
- House Cherry (see recipe on p. 56), for garnish

1. In a cocktail shaker filled with ice, combine all of the ingredients except the House Cherry and shake until well combined and very cold. Strain the cocktail into an iced rocks glass. Garnish with the House Cherry and serve.

Baked Pita Chips with Creamy Cashew Pesto Dip

These are two excellent snacks. The Creamy Cashew Pesto Dip can also be used as a rich filling for stuffed shells, ravioli, or pretty much anything that can be stuffed! Enjoy the Baked Pita Chips alongside the Sir Thomas with Earl Grey Syrup (see recipe on p. 64).

YIELD: **1 cup (65 g) Pita Chip Seasoning; 3–4 cups (672–896 g) Baked Pita Chips**

For the Pita Chip Seasoning:

- ¼ cup (14 g) dried parsley
- 2 tablespoons sea salt (use half this quantity if using pink Himalayan salt instead)
- 2 tablespoons dried bell pepper (you may have to chop if it comes in large pieces)
- 2 tablespoons dried onion
- 1¼ tablespoons dried basil
- ¾ teaspoon garlic powder
- ¼ teaspoon dried thyme
- ⅛ teaspoon dried lemon peel
- ⅛ teaspoon dried dill weed
- Dash celery seed

For the Baked Pita Chips:

- 1 package whole wheat pita bread
- ¼ cup (59 mL) plus 1 tablespoon extra virgin olive oil, divided
- 3 tablespoons (42 g) Pita Chip Seasoning
- 2 cups (474 mL) Creamy Cashew Pesto Dip (see recipe on p. 63), for serving

To make the Seasoning:

1. In a small mixing bowl, stir all of the ingredients together thoroughly with a small whisk or fork. Use immediately or store in an airtight container for up to 3 months.

To make the Baked Pita Chips:

1. Preheat the oven to 375°F (190°C). Line a baking sheet with parchment paper.

2. Separate the pita bread into 2 stacks. Slice each stack in half, and then slice each again into quarters so that each slice of pita bread yields 8 wedges. Place the pita bread back in its bag.

3. Add the ¼ cup (59 mL) oil to the bag. Tightly twist shut the top of the bag and gently toss the pita bread slices with the oil. Add the Pita Chip Seasoning and shake again gently until all the slices are well covered with oil and seasoning. Add more oil and seasoning, if needed, to fully coat the pita.

4. Place the slices on the prepared baking sheet. Bake for 15 to 20 minutes, or until the pieces are crispy and golden brown. Make sure to turn them about halfway through the cooking time; at that time, you may wish to use the remaining 1 tablespoon oil to brush some of the slices with a little more oil. Serve with the Creamy Cashew Pesto Dip.

COOKS' NOTE: You can also use the Pita Chip Seasoning as a roasted veggie marinade by adding ½ cup (119 mL) olive oil. In a large mixing bowl, add the Seasoning to the oil and toss in 4 to 6 cups (600–900 g) of any mixture of sliced vegetables. Roast the vegetables on a parchment-lined baking sheet at 425°F (220°C) for 15 to 20 minutes depending on the size and thickness of the vegetables you've chosen.

Creamy Cashew Pesto Dip

This is a great summer recipe for Midwest dwellers, who can find mighty branches of fresh basil at farmers' markets everywhere in July through September.

YIELD: **2¼ cups (310 g)**

- 2 cups (276 g) raw cashews
- 9½ cups (228 g) fresh basil
- ¾ cup (168 g) nutritional yeast flakes
- 3 tablespoons (45 mL) olive oil
- 2 tablespoons dried onion
- 1 tablespoon chopped fresh parsley
- 2 teaspoons sea salt
- ½ teaspoon dried thyme
- Freshly ground black pepper, to taste

1. In a medium mixing bowl, cover the cashews in water. Allow them to soak for 30 to 60 minutes. Drain all but 2 tablespoons of the soaking water. Reserve the 2 tablespoons soaking water.

2. Place all of the ingredients, including the soaking water, in the bowl of a food processor fitted with the metal "S" blade and blend until smooth, scraping the sides often with a rubber spatula. (Depending on the capacity of your food processor's bowl, you may need to add the basil in 2- to 3-cup intervals.) Serve immediately or store in an airtight container in the refrigerator for up to 5 to 7 days. If the top turns brown, simply skim off and stir as you would guacamole.

COOKS' NOTE: Looking to reduce the amount of oil you use when cooking? Consider replacing some of the oil used in recipes that call for soaking nuts with some of the nuts' soaking water.

VARIATIONS: Consider topping the Creamy Cashew Pesto Dip with scallions, roasted red peppers, or kalamata olives.

If you want to use less basil, use 5½ cups basil mixed with 4 cups baby spinach leaves.

Sir Thomas with Earl Grey Simple Syrup

Most gin experts agree: Now is the best time in centuries to be drinking one of the world's oldest spirits. Gin is an urbane elixir; some suggest it infuses all the virtues and vices of urban life in its lovely juniper bouquet.

Since we dwell in one of America's greatest cities, we had to create our own twist on that classic gin concoction, the Tom Collins. We combine a locally distilled gin with our own Earl Grey tea-infused simple syrup, fresh lemon juice, and a splash of seltzer. The result is a sweet and satisfying cocktail that leaves you feeling refreshed, yet warmed from within.

YIELD: **1 cocktail; 12 ounces (360 mL) Earl Grey Simple Syrup**

For the Earl Grey Simple Syrup:

- **1 cup (237 mL) filtered water, heated**
- **3 Earl Grey tea bags**
- **1 cup (200g) organic granulated cane sugar**

For the Cocktail:

- **1½ ounces (45 mL) dry botanical gin (we use Letherbee London Dry)**
- **1 ounce (30 mL) Earl Grey Simple Syrup**
- **½ ounce (15 mL) fresh lemon juice**
- **Sparkling water, for topping**
- **Lemon wheel, for garnish**

To make the Earl Grey Simple Syrup:

1. Make a strong tea with the hot water and tea bags. Press the tea bags and remove.

2. Place the brewed tea and sugar in a small saucepan over medium-low heat. Cook, stirring constantly, for 15 minutes, until the sugar has dissolved. Let cool. Store in an air-tight container in the refrigerator for up to 2 weeks.

To make the Cocktail:

1. In an iced Collins glass, build all of the ingredients except the water and the lemon wheel. Top with the sparkling water and serve garnished with the lemon wheel.

IMBIBERS' NOTE: If you don't want to make your own Earl Grey Simple Syrup, try adding splashes of black tea and agave nectar to the drink instead.

Mexican Dark Chocolate Bark

Every party needs a little something sweet. This recipe is a great way to impress your friends by making them homemade chocolates. It's a lot easier than it sounds! This recipe is inspired by the fresh cayenne peppers available in the Great Lakes region at summer's end. This sweet, savory, spicy snack goes excellently with the rich and creamy spices of the Calcutta Connection (recipe follows).

YIELD: **8 cups (915 g) chocolate bark**

- **24 ounces (678 g) pure unsweetened cacao bars (70% cacao or higher—the purer, the better)**
- **2 fresh cayenne peppers, minced or puréed**
- **½ teaspoon ground cinnamon**
- **1 cup (237 mL) pure maple syrup**
- **2 cups (256 g) raw pepitas (pumpkin seeds)**
- **Coarse sea salt, for sprinkling**

1. Place a double boiler over medium-low heat. Boil the water. Break up the cacao bars into 1-inch (2.5-cm) pieces and place the pieces in the double boiler. (If you don't have a double boiler, you can place a small saucepan inside another saucepan with 1 inch (2.5 cm) of simmering water in it. Just make sure the water does not touch the upper pan, and that no water comes in contact with the cacao.)

2. Once the cacao begins to melt, stir in the peppers and cinnamon with a wooden spoon. Then, slowly add the maple syrup by drizzling it into the mixture. Continue stirring; the mixture will become extremely thick, like fudge. At this point, use a whisk to continue mixing to ensure that the mixture is thoroughly combined. Continue to cook the mixture over medium-low heat for another 10 minutes. Remove from the heat.

3. Cut 2 sheets of parchment paper sized to fit in a baking sheet. Using a silicone spatula, scrape the chocolate mixture onto a sheet of the parchment paper and then cover with the second sheet. Use a rolling pin and some elbow grease to flatten the chocolate out evenly until the chocolate mixture is about a centimeter (half an inch) thick throughout.

4. Place the chocolate-covered parchment paper on the baking sheet. Sprinkle with the pepitas and lightly sprinkle with coarse sea salt. (You may have to press down on the pepitas a bit.)

5. Refrigerate for 30 to 45 minutes, until firm. Using clean or gloved hands, break the chilled chocolate bark into 1-inch (2.5-cm) pieces and either serve, bag to use as gifts, or store in airtight containers. Keep refrigerated for up to 2 weeks or freeze for up to 2 months.

COOKS' NOTE: When handling hot peppers, it is advisable to wear rubber gloves as the oils penetrate your skin and linger for hours. Make sure that you do not touch your eyes after handling hot peppers. Depending on the thickness of your chocolate, you may need to use a knife to cut it into squares.

Calcutta Connection

Here's a brilliant idea: Pair the delicious flavors of chai with spiced rum! In this drink, the tropics mix and mingle with the tea's eastern spices. We had these items already in the pantry and started thinking about ways to put them to good use. Taking what you already have at home and making something new out of it by pairing the ingredients together in a different way often yields fantastic results. You save money, nurture your creativity, and possibly create some kitchen magic at the same time!

YIELD: **1 cocktail**

- 1½ ounces (45 mL) spiced rum (we prefer Kraken)
- 1½ ounces (45 mL) coconut milk
- 1 ounce (30 mL) Masala Chai concentrate (we use the Rishi brand) or any strong, sweet chai tea
- Cinnamon stick, for garnish

1. Place a rocks glass in the freezer for 10 minutes.

2. In a cocktail shaker filled with ice, combine all of the ingredients except the cinnamon stick and shake until well combined and very cold. Strain the cocktail into the chilled rocks glass. Garnish with the cinnamon stick and serve.

Salads, Dressings, and Condiments

Salads are a versatile way to make use of the best produce available in your area to create a terrific snack or meal in a snap. As a main dish, they're the perfect one-dish meal. Throw everything in a bowl, whip up some dressing, and hit the road. You can always add potatoes, beans, and grains to make your salad heartier. The sky's the limit when it comes to salads, so release the rabbit within you!

PICTURED: **Taco Salad (p. 76)**

Arugula Salad with Cranberries and Pear

This salad is perfect for the heat of late summer. You can probably source arugula and pears locally that time of year. This salad's a light combination of sweet and savory flavors.

YIELD: **6 side salads**

- 8 cups (240 g) arugula
- ½ red onion, thinly sliced
- ½–1 cup (119–237 mL) Cranberry Balsamic Vinaigrette Dressing (recipe follows) or a citrus-based dressing
- 4 pears, thinly sliced (you can use seasonal berries or even apples in the fall)
- 1 cup (112 g) dried cranberries
- ⅓ cup (36 g) coarsely chopped pecans (optional)
- Freshly ground black pepper, to taste

1. In a large mixing bowl, toss the arugula and red onion with the Cranberry Balsamic Vinaigrette Dressing until well coated.

2. Top the salad with the pears, cranberries, and pecans (if using). Toss again. Sprinkle with the black pepper. Serve in small bowls.

Cranberry Balsamic Vinaigrette Dressing

YIELD: **1½ cups (356 mL)**

- ½ cup (119 mL) white balsamic vinegar
- ½ cup (119 mL) whole cranberry sauce
- ¼ teaspoon sea salt
- ⅛ teaspoon freshly ground black pepper
- ¾ cup (178 mL) extra virgin olive oil

1. In the bowl of a food processor fitted with the metal "S" blade or a blender, combine the balsamic vinegar, cranberry sauce, salt, and pepper and process until smooth.

2. As the processor is running, slowly pour in the oil, creating an emulsion. Use immediately or store in a container or jar for 1 week in the refrigerator. Shake well before serving after storage.

Simple Kale Salad

Kale is packed with calcium and iron, so it's a wonderful green to incorporate into your diet. Switch out the tomatoes and seeds called for in the recipe with whatever veggies and protein sources that are comparable in color and available in your area. Here, we've paired this hardy yet simple salad with our creamy Tahini Dressing (recipe follows), but it's also delicious with Chicago Diner Vegan Ranch Dressing (see recipe on p. 73) or our House Balsamic Vinaigrette (see recipe on p. 79). Be sure you put the salad together about half a day before serving, because the kale leaves will need to soften from contact with the dressing.

YIELD: **6 side salads**

- 1 bunch organic kale
- 4 heirloom tomatoes, cut into cubes (about 2 cups [380 g])
- ¼ cup (38 g) finely chopped red onion
- ⅓ cup (47 g) hemp or sunflower seeds
- ½ cup (119 mL) Tahini Dressing (recipe follows)

1. Rinse the kale and pat it dry with a paper towel. Remove the kale stalks, tear the leaves into half inch pieces, and dry in a salad spinner to wick away any excess moisture. Massage the leaves gently to bring out their full color and nutrients.

2. In a large serving bowl, combine the kale, tomatoes, red onion, and seeds and toss well.

3. Add the Tahini Dressing 4 to 6 hours before serving in order to soften the leaves. Toss well and store in the refrigerator until serving. Serve in small bowls.

COOKS' NOTE: Use other veggies as they are seasonally available. Try to maintain a color variety for aesthetic and nutritional balance.

Tahini Dressing

YIELD: **1¼ cups (296 mL)**

- **⅔ cup (165 g) tahini (raw or roasted)**
- **3 cloves garlic, minced**
- **Juice of ½ lemon**
- **2 tablespoons finely chopped fresh flat-leaf parsley**
- **¾ teaspoon sea salt**
- **½ teaspoon ground cumin**
- **¼–½ teaspoon cayenne pepper, or to taste (optional)**
- **Freshly ground black pepper, to taste**
- **¼ cup (59 mL) plus 1 tablespoon water, or as needed**

1. In a small mixing bowl, whisk together all of the ingredients except the water.

2. Slowly add the water, 1 tablespoon at a time, while whisking constantly. Keep in mind that Tahini Dressing thickens over time, so you may want to add a little more water than you initially think. Add the water until you feel the dressing has reached the right consistency and taste for your needs. Use immediately or store in a jar for 2 weeks in the refrigerator. Shake well before serving after storage.

COOKS' NOTE: If you use roasted tahini, you'll need to use more water than you would with raw tahini. The amount of water really varies depending on the brand of tahini you choose, so just try adding 1 to 2 tablespoons at a time until the desired consistency is reached.

You may substitute lime in any recipe that calls for lemon.

Red and Green Salad

A great way to take advantage of seasonal produce is to use different locally sourced lettuces. This salad really showcases the bounty of the late summer/early fall harvest in the Great Lakes region.

YIELD: 6 side salads

- 1 small head red leaf lettuce (about 3 cups [108 g])
- ½ head savoy cabbage (about 3 cups [210 g])
- 1 cup (30 g) arugula, finely chopped
- 1 pint (300 g) heirloom cherry tomatoes, halved
- 2 cups (220 g) organic carrots, shredded
- 1 cup (116 g) radishes, thinly sliced
- ½ cup (24 g) fresh chives, minced
- ½ cup (119 mL) Chicago Diner Vegan Ranch Dressing (recipe follows)

1. Thoroughly wash and dry the lettuce and vegetables.

2. Tear the lettuce into 1-inch (2.5-cm) pieces. Slice the cabbage into long strips and then halve them again so they are about 1 inch (2.5 cm) long. Use a salad spinner to wick all the moisture from the lettuce, cabbage, and arugula.

3. In a large mixing bowl, toss together all of the ingredients except the dressing using clean hands or tongs. Serve in small bowls with the Chicago Diner Vegan Ranch Dressing or the vinaigrette of your choice.

COOKS' NOTES: Try this with unique varieties of vegetables like red oakleaf lettuce, famosa cabbage, and French breakfast radishes. If possible, visit your local farmers' market to find these delightful tastes of the season.

If arugula is not available, substitute mache lettuce. You can substitute parsnips for the tomatoes, as well—or any other garden wonders that come into season.

Chicago Diner Vegan Ranch Dressing

Ranch dressing is an American classic, so of course we've taken it upon ourselves to come up with a veggie-friendly version. This goes great on anything!

YIELD: **1¼ cups (296 mL)**

- **1 cup (224 g) vegan mayonnaise (we like Vegenaise)***
- **3 tablespoons (45 mL) soy milk, or as needed**
- **1 tablespoon dried parsley**
- **1½ teaspoons apple cider vinegar**
- **1 teaspoon fresh lemon juice**
- **1 teaspoon dried dill**
- **1 teaspoon onion powder**
- **1 teaspoon dried garlic**
- **Sea salt and freshly ground black pepper, to taste**

1. In a small mixing bowl, whisk together all of the ingredients until smooth and creamy. Adjust the soy milk quantity depending on your preference for the dressing's consistency. Use immediately or store in a container or jar for 2 weeks in the refrigerator. Shake well before serving after storage.

---

* If you can't find vegan mayonnaise in your area, combine ⅓ cup (78 g) silken tofu and ⅔ cup (158 mL) soy milk in a blender and purée until smooth.

Tempeh Caesar Salad

We serve this salad at the Diner with either seasoned tempeh or Seitan Chickun (see recipe on p. 22). Either way, it's a delicious and filling entrée. You'll love this salad in the summertime, paired with a nice glass of white wine!

YIELD: **2 entrée salads**

- 8 Hickory-Marinated Tempeh strips (see recipe on p. 21)
- ¾ cup (169 g) quartered artichoke hearts
- 2 Roma tomatoes, cut into wedges
- 3 cups (108 g) chopped romaine lettuce
- ⅔ cup (20 g) croutons (optional)
- ¼ cup (30 g) chopped roasted red peppers
- 1 cup (237 mL) Dijon Caesar Dressing (recipe follows)

1. Marinate and pan fry the Hickory-Marinated Tempeh according to the recipe. When the Hickory-Marinated Tempeh is almost done, toss in the artichokes for 1 to 2 minutes to brown them a bit. Remove from the heat and set aside.

2. Place all of the ingredients except the Hickory-Marinated Tempeh in a large salad bowl and toss with the Dijon Caesar Dressing. Using tongs, fill 2 entrée-sized salad bowls with the salad. Top with the Hickory-Marinated Tempeh and serve.

Dijon Caesar Dressing

YIELD: **1 cup (237 mL)**

- ⅔ cup (149 g) vegan mayonnaise (we like Vegenaise)*
- 2 cloves garlic, minced
- 2 teaspoons Dijon mustard
- 2 teaspoons extra virgin olive oil
- 1 teaspoon white wine vinegar
- ½ teaspoon fresh lemon juice
- ¼ teaspoon sea salt or more, to taste
- ¼ teaspoon freshly ground black pepper

1. In a blender, combine all of the ingredients and purée until the mixture is smooth and creamy. Use immediately or store in a container or jar for 2 weeks in the refrigerator. Shake well before serving after storage.

* If you can't find vegan mayonnaise in your area, combine ⅓ cup (78 g) silken tofu and ⅔ cup (158 mL) soy milk in a blender and purée until smooth.

Taco Salad

This Tex-Mex classic is our best-selling salad. If you lived through the 1980s, chances are that at some point, you've been served a taco salad in a deep-fried tortilla bowl. We've done away with that and put a contemporary spin on this satisfying salad.

YIELD: 2 entrée salads

- 3 cups (108 g) mixed salad greens (we suggest an organic spring mix)
- 1 cup (172 g) black beans
- 1 cup (160 g) sweet corn
- ½ cup 116 g) vegan chorizo
- ½ cup (56 g) vegan Cheddar cheese
- ½ cup (75 g) diced onion
- ½ cup (80 g) diced tomato
- ¼ cup (25 g) diced fresh jalapeño pepper
- ½ cup (119 mL) Southwest Spice Dressing (recipe follows)
- Organic tortilla chips, for garnish
- ¼ cup (59 mL) vegan sour cream (we like Tofutti), for garnish
- ½ avocado, sliced, for garnish

1. In a large mixing bowl, toss together the greens, beans, corn, vegan chorizo, vegan Cheddar shreds, onion, tomato, and jalapeño pepper.

2. Dress the salad with the Southwest Spice Dressing. Toss well.

3. Line 4 entrée-sized salad bowls with the chips. Fill them with 4 equal portions of the salad and garnish with the vegan sour cream and avocado. Serve immediately.

Southwest Spice Dressing

YIELD: 1¼ cups (296 mL)

- 1 cup (224 g) vegan mayonnaise (we like Vegenaise)*
- 1 tablespoon fresh salsa
- 1 tablespoon fresh lime juice
- 1 tablespoon Sriracha sauce
- 2½ teaspoons onion powder
- 2 teaspoons fresh cilantro, finely chopped
- 1 teaspoon organic granulated cane sugar (optional)
- ½ teaspoon ground cumin
- ½ teaspoon chili powder
- Dash cayenne pepper

1. In a blender, combine all of the ingredients and purée until the mixture is smooth and creamy. Use immediately or store in a container or jar for 2 weeks in the refrigerator. Shake well before serving after storage.

* If you can't find vegan mayonnaise in your area, combine ⅓ cup (78 g) silken tofu and ⅔ cup (158 mL) soy milk in a blender and purée until smooth.

Quinoa Tabouleh

Tabouleh is always a delight, especially in the summertime. Its simple citrus and mint flavors are refreshing on a sandwich, grilled veggie burger, or all on its own. In this recipe, the ancient, protein-packed seed quinoa is a great substitute for tabouleh's traditional basis, bulgur wheat. The art of improvisation is essential when coming up with new and exciting favorites.

YIELD: 4 (1-cup [179-g]) servings

- 1 cup (179 g) quinoa, thoroughly rinsed
- 1½ cups (356 mL) Vegetable Stock (see recipe on p. 93)
- 2–3 Roma tomatoes, seeded and diced
- 1 medium cucumber, peeled, seeded, and diced
- 2 green onions, chopped
- 1½ cups (45 g) loosely chopped fresh flat-leaf parsley
- ¼ cup (59 mL) extra virgin olive oil
- ¼ cup (59 mL) fresh lemon juice, or to taste
- 2 tablespoons chopped fresh mint, or to taste
- 1 teaspoon sea salt, or to taste
- ¼ teaspoon freshly ground black pepper, or to taste

1. Follow the package directions to prepare the quinoa, but instead of water, use the Vegetable Stock. Remove from the heat. Set the quinoa aside and allow it to cool completely.

2. In a large mixing bowl, combine all of the ingredients and toss well, adjusting the quantities of the last 4 ingredients to taste.

3. Serve in small bowls or as a side item or topping for sandwiches, burgers, and almost any other entrée.

COOKS' NOTE: In lieu of vegetable stock, you can always use a vegetable bouillon cube dissolved in water. If you are cooking 1 cup (179 g) or less of a particular grain, we suggest using ½ a cube for each 1 to 2 cups (237–474 mL) of water.

Farro Salad

Farro is an ancient grain believed to have sustained the legions of the Roman Empire. This salad really shows off the grain's complex, nutty flavors.

YIELD: **4 side salads**

- 1¼ cups (296 mL) Vegetable Stock (see recipe on p. 93)
- ½ cup (50 g) farro, rinsed well
- 1 small red pepper, julienned
- 2 scallions, cut on an angle
- ½ cup (73 g) fresh green peas
- ¼–½ cup (59–119 mL) House Balsamic Vinaigrette (recipe follows)
- ⅓ cup (38 g) coarsely chopped toasted walnuts
- ¼ cup (28 g) dried cherries or other dried fruit
- ½ cup (15 g) chopped fresh flat-leaf parsley
- ½ teaspoon sea salt
- ¼ teaspoon freshly ground black pepper
- Salad greens, for serving

1. In a large saucepan over medium heat, combine the Vegetable Stock and farro. Bring the mixture to a boil. Reduce the heat to low, cover, and simmer for 25 to 30 minutes, or until tender. Remove from the heat and drain any remaining liquid. Set the farro aside to cool completely.

2. Once the farro has completely cooled, toss all of the ingredients except the salad greens together in a large mixing bowl.

3. Serve in small bowls, each on a bed of the salad greens.

COOKS' NOTE: In lieu of vegetable stock, you can always use a vegetable bouillon cube dissolved in water. If you are cooking 1 cup (179 g) or less of a particular grain, we suggest using ½ a cube for each 1 to 2 cups (237–474 mL) of water.

VARIATION: If you don't have farro on hand, try this recipe with barley.

House Balsamic Vinaigrette

This is our basic house balsamic dressing. We serve it on everything from our Portobello Quinoa Salad to simple side salads. It's great to always have a basic balsamic dressing ready to serve. Once you get the hang of this recipe, you can play around with it, substituting the recipe's dried herbs with fresh ones or maybe even tossing in some whole-grain mustard.

YIELD: ¾ cup (178 mL)

- ¼ cup (59 mL) balsamic vinegar
- 1 tablespoon dried basil
- 2–3 teaspoons organic granulated cane sugar
- ¾ teaspoon dried onion
- ½ teaspoon dried garlic or 1 minced clove garlic
- ½ cup (119 mL) extra virgin olive oil

1. In the bowl of a food processor fitted with the metal "S" blade or a blender, combine all of the ingredients except the oil and process until smooth.

2. As the processor is running, slowly pour in the oil, creating an emulsion. Use immediately or store in a container or jar for 2 weeks in the refrigerator. Shake well before serving after storage.

French Lentil Salad

Some argue that the French lentil is the tastiest of all lentils because of its peppery tones. It can take longer to cook than other lentils, but it's well worth the wait. We've taken the French theme a step further by tossing it together with a whole-grain Mustard Vinaigrette.

YIELD: **4–6 servings**

- **1 cup (192 g) dry French lentils**
- **5–6 cups (1.19–1.42 L) water**
- **1 thyme sprig**
- **1 large red pepper**
- **1 medium white or yellow onion, peeled**
- **Extra virgin olive oil, for brushing**
- **2 cups (260 g) sliced cucumber**
- **¼–½ cup (59–119 mL) Mustard Vinaigrette (recipe follows)**
- **Baby spinach leaves, for serving**
- **Lemon wedge**
- **Scallions or chives, for garnish**

1. Preheat the oven to 350°F (180°C). Line a baking sheet with parchment paper.

2. In a medium stockpot over medium heat, bring the lentils, water, and thyme sprig to a boil. Reduce the heat to low and simmer for 20 to 30 minutes, until the lentils are tender. Remove from the heat, drain the lentils, and place them in a large serving bowl to cool.

3. Place the pepper and onion on the baking sheet and brush them with the oil. Bake for 20 to 25 minutes, or until soft. Remove from the oven and set aside to cool.

4. Once the pepper and onion have cooled, peel, seed, and slice the pepper, and slice the onion.

5. Combine all of the ingredients except the lemon wedge, spinach, and scallions in the bowl containing the lentils. Toss well with the Mustard Vinaigrette until thoroughly combined.

6. Line a serving bowl with a bed of the spinach. Place the lentil salad on the bed of spinach. Drizzle with the juice of the lemon wedge and garnish with the scallions or chives. Serve.

COOKS' NOTE: This salad is actually best after it's had a chance to marinate for a day, but let it come back to room temperature before serving.

Mustard Vinaigrette

YIELD: ¾ cup (178 mL)

- ½ cup (119 mL) extra virgin olive oil
- 2 tablespoons white wine vinegar
- 2 tablespoons whole-grain mustard
- Freshly ground black pepper, to taste
- Sea salt, to taste

1. Place all of the ingredients in a jar or salad shaker and shake vigorously until fully emulsified. Use immediately or store in a container or jar for 2 weeks in the refrigerator. Shake well before serving after storage.

Waldorf Salad

This is about as classic American as a salad can get. According to legend, it was invented at New York's Waldorf Hotel (now the Waldorf Astoria) in the 1890s. Our creative culinary team came up with this version in the spring of 2013, and diners rejoiced!

YIELD: **4 entrée salads**

For the Waldorf Dressing:

- ½ cup (112 g) vegan mayonnaise (we like Vegenaise)*
- ¼ cup (59 mL) vegan sour cream
- Generous ½ teaspoon agave nectar
- ½ teaspoon fresh lemon juice
- ¼ teaspoon curry powder
- Sea salt and freshly ground black pepper, to taste
- 1 tablespoon finely chopped fresh flat-leaf parsley

For the Waldorf Salads:

- 1½ cups (188 g) thinly sliced Golden Delicious apples
- 1½ cups (180 g) sliced celery
- 1 cup (100 g) halved red grapes
- ¼ cup (25 g) halved walnuts
- 5 cups (150 g) baby spinach, for serving

To make the Waldorf Dressing:

1. In a blender or the bowl of a food processor fitted with the metal "S" blade, purée together all of the ingredients except the parsley.

2. Once the mixture is smooth and creamy, transfer to a bowl and fold in the parsley. Set aside.

To make the Waldorf Salads:

1. In a large mixing bowl, toss the apples, celery, grapes, and walnuts with the Waldorf Dressing.

2. Place 4 small salad bowls on the counter and line each with 1¼ cups (37.5 g) baby spinach. Top each with a generous spoonful of the salad mixture. Serve.

---

* If you can't find vegan mayonnaise in your area, combine ⅓ cup (78 g) silken tofu and ⅔ cup (158 mL) soy milk in a blender and purée until smooth.

COOKS' NOTE: At the restaurant, we use an immersion blender to make all of our creamy dressings, but it isn't always the best tool for home use because of the relatively small quantities needed. Try a blender or food processor fitted with the metal "S" blade, or apply some veggie-powered muscle using a good, sturdy whisk.

TIME SAVER: The dressing recipe makes enough for 2 batches, which really comes in handy if you get invited to an impromptu dinner party, brunch, or summer cookout.

More Dressings!

CLOCKWISE FROM TOP LEFT:
Ranch Dressing (p. 73), Balsamic Vinaigrette (p. 79), and Thousand Island Dressing (p. 112)

Roasted Red Pepper Dressing

This dressing is what Jo and Mickey refer to as SOS—free of salt, oil, and sugar, yet packed with flavor. Toss it on your favorite salad.

YIELD: **1 cup (237 mL)**

- 2 large red peppers, halved, stemmed, and seeded*
- 3–4 large cloves garlic
- ⅓ cup (79 mL) rice wine vinegar
- ¼ cup (59 mL) water
- 1 teaspoon fresh oregano leaves
- Dash freshly ground black pepper

1. Preheat the oven to 350°F (180°C). Line a baking sheet with parchment paper.

2. Place the peppers and garlic on the baking sheet. Bake for 20 to 25 minutes, or until soft. Remove from the oven and set aside to cool.

3. Once the peppers and garlic have cooled, place them in a blender with the remaining ingredients and purée until smooth. Use immediately or store for up to 2 weeks in the refrigerator. Shake well before serving.

Asian Dressing

This aromatic dressing isn't just for salads! It's also great with grilled tofu or noodles.

YIELD: **1 cup (237 mL)**

- 1 teaspoon sesame seeds
- ⅓ cup (79 mL) rice wine vinegar
- ¼ cup (59 mL) sesame oil
- 2 tablespoons mirin rice wine
- 1 teaspoon sea salt
- ½ teaspoon freshly ground black pepper
- ½ teaspoon freshly grated ginger

1. In a small dry pan over medium heat, warm and toss the sesame seeds for 1 to 2 minutes. (Be very careful to toast, and not burn, the seeds.) Remove from the heat.

2. In a small bowl, whisk together all of the ingredients. Use immediately or store in a container or jar for 1 week in the refrigerator. Shake well before serving after storage.

Poppyseed Dressing

Everybody loves a sweet dressing now and then. This one is great in the summertime over baby spinach and fresh seasonal berries.

YIELD: **¾ cup (178 mL)**

- ½ cup (119 mL) vegetable oil
- ¼ cup (59 mL) apple cider vinegar
- 2 tablespoons agave nectar
- ½ tablespoon chopped onion
- 1 teaspoon dry ground mustard
- ½ teaspoon poppyseeds
- ¼ teaspoon sea salt

1. In a blender, combine all of the ingredients and purée until the mixture becomes white, smooth, and creamy. Use immediately or store in a container or jar for 1 week in the refrigerator. Shake well before serving after storage.

---

* Actually, any color of pepper works fine in this recipe! You might also want to consider adding a little sweet onion to the mix. Improvise and get creative with what you have!

Condiments

CLOCKWISE FROM TOP LEFT:
Raw Pumpkin Seed Mayonnaise (pg. 86), Fire-Roasted Salsa (pg. 87), and Chimichurri Sauce (pg. 90)

Raw Sauerkraut

Fermented foods like sauerkraut and tempeh aid in digestion and help support the immune system. Making your own is an affordable, quick, and easy way to always have homemade condiments within reach. Add this delicious sauerkraut to sandwiches and salads.

YIELD: **1 (32-ounce [908-g]) jar**

- **1 medium-sized head of green cabbage (red works too!)**
- **1½ tablespoons sea salt**
- **1 tablespoon caraway seeds (optional)**

1. In the bowl of a food processor fitted with the shredding blade, finely shred the cabbage.

2. Place the cabbage in a large mixing bowl and dust it with the salt.

3. Using very clean or gloved hands, massage the salt into the cabbage for 3 to 5 minutes, or until you can feel the cabbage's fibers begin to break down. (This is known as a "salt cook" method.) Add the caraway seeds, if using. Drain the cabbage, reserving all the liquid.

4. Place the cabbage in a sterilized canning jar. Press it down very firmly, until it fills only about ¾ of the jar.

5. Pour the reserved liquid over the cabbage. Cover the jar with cheesecloth and seal its lid. Set the jar on the counter, away from sunlight, for 3 days before using. Store for up to 3 weeks in the refrigerator.

Raw Pumpkin Seed Mayonnaise

Hats off to Chef Jo for coming up with this creative condiment! It's excellent as a sandwich spread, paired with raw veggies, or added to Crostini (see recipe on p. 60).

YIELD: **1½ cups (356 mL)**

- **1 cup (128 g) raw pumpkin seeds, soaked overnight**
- **½ cup (119 mL) sunflower oil**
- **1 clove garlic**
- **2 teaspoons organic apple cider vinegar**
- **1 teaspoon onion powder**
- **1 teaspoon curry powder**
- **¾ teaspoon sea salt**
- **¼ teaspoon ground turmeric**

1. In a blender, combine all of the ingredients and purée until the mixture becomes smooth and creamy. Use immediately or store in a container or jar for 1 week in the refrigerator. Shake well before serving after storage.

Fire-Roasted Salsa

You can bring on the heat with this salsa recipe, which first hit our menu in the spring of 2013.

YIELD: **2 cups (474 mL)**

- **2 tablespoons canola or grapeseed oil**
- **¼ onion, chopped**
- **7 cloves garlic, minced**
- **5 Roma tomatoes, chopped**
- **⅓ fresh jalapeño pepper, minced**
- **¼–½ cup (4–8 g) chopped fresh cilantro**
- **½ chipotle pepper in adobo sauce (canned)**
- **Juice of ½ lime**
- **½ teaspoon ground cumin**
- **½ teaspoon sea salt, or to taste**
- **½ teaspoon freshly ground black pepper**

1. In a large frying pan over medium heat, warm the oil. Add the onion, garlic, tomatoes, and jalapeño pepper and sauté for 5 to 10 minutes, until the mixture browns and even starts to burn just a little bit. Remove from the heat.

2. Remove the mixture from the pan and place it in the bowl of a food processor fitted with the metal "S" blade. Reserve the oil in the pan.

3. To the same oiled frying pan, add the cilantro. Return the pan to medium heat. Char the cilantro a bit and then remove the pan from the heat. Remove the cilantro from the pan and reserve in a small bowl. Pour the oil from the pan, as well as all the remaining ingredients except the cilantro, into the food processor.

4. Pulse the mixture until it is chunky. Add the cilantro and pulse 1 to 2 more times. Serve immediately in a small serving bowl or place the salsa in a glass jar and refrigerate. The salsa will remain fresh for 5 to 7 days.

COOKS' NOTE: In a pinch, you can use 1 can of fire-roasted tomatoes (we like the Muir Glen brand) instead of the Roma tomatoes. Fire-roasted tomatoes are also delicious in our Quinoa Chili (see recipe on p. 94).

Tomatillo Salsa

Tomatillos are a delight when properly prepared. Here's a simple and delicious recipe for this Mexican staple.

YIELD: **2 cups (474 mL)**

- **1 pound (454 g) tomatillos, husked**
- **1 clove garlic**
- **2–3 jalapeño peppers or 1 serrano pepper**
- **⅔ cup (158 mL) water**
- **½ cup (75 g) chopped yellow onion**
- **1 teaspoon ground cumin**
- **½ teaspoon sea salt**
- **¼ cup (4 g) chopped fresh cilantro**

1. Preheat the oven to 350°F (180°C). Line a baking sheet with parchment paper.

2. Place the tomatillos, garlic, and peppers on the baking sheet. Bake for 15 to 20 minutes, or until soft. Remove from the oven and set aside to cool.

3. Once the tomatillos have cooled, remove their skins.

4. In the bowl of a food processor fitted with the metal "S" blade or blender, place all of the ingredients except the cilantro. Pulse a few times. Add the cilantro and pulse a few more times. This is a chunky salsa, so beware of overblending. Serve immediately in a small serving bowl or place the salsa in a sealed glass jar and refrigerate for 5 to 7 days.

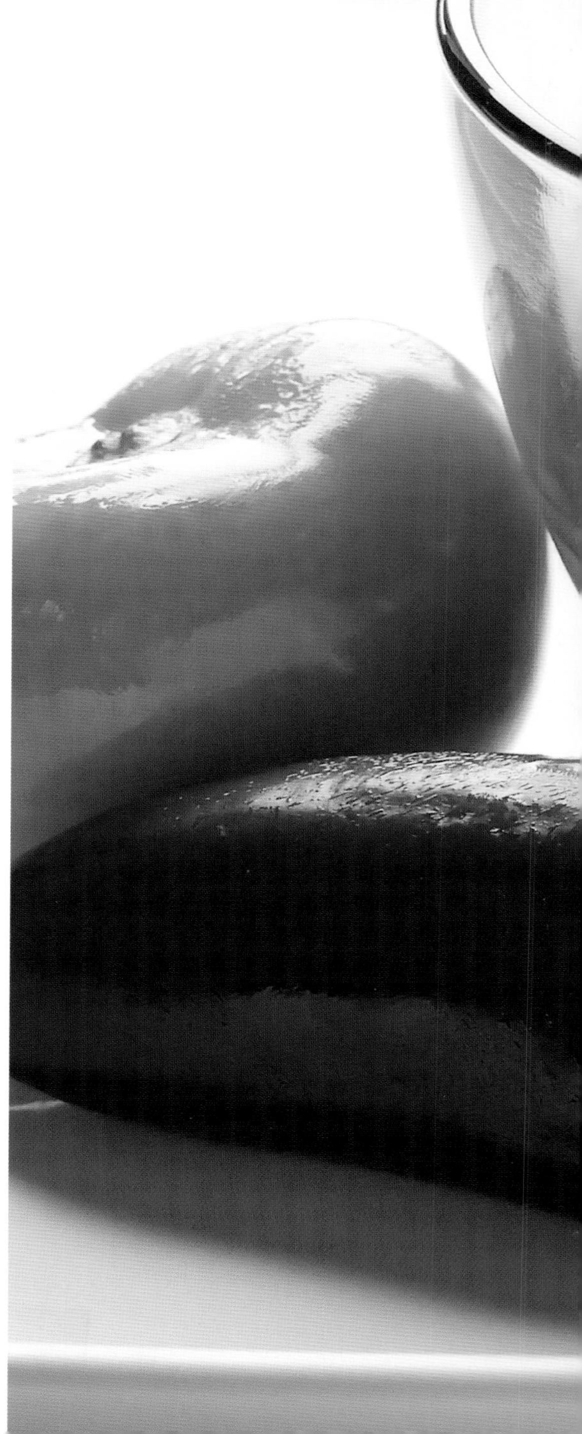

Sweet and Sour Lemon Chutney

This brunch condiment adds a yummy citrus splash to a range of dishes. Take it with you on picnics for spreading on crackers, toast, or biscuits, and as a condiment for curried dishes.

YIELD: **1½ cups (356 mL) chutney**

- 2 large organic lemons, skin on and diced
- ⅓ cup (67 g) + 2½ tablespoons organic granulated cane sugar
- 2 tablespoons fresh organic lemon juice
- ½ teaspoon ground turmeric
- 2½ teaspoons sea salt
- 1 teaspoon ground cayenne pepper

1. Cut the lemons into thin slices and then cube the slices.

2. In a small saucepan over medium-low heat, combine all of the ingredients. Allow the mixture to reach a simmer and cook for 5 to 6 minutes. Remove from the heat. The chutney should be slightly thick; it will thicken more as it cools.

3. Pour the chutney into a sanitized Mason jar. Seal it and store it at room temperature for 5 days before using. Serve, store in the refrigerator for up to 3 months, or give as a gift.

Chimichurri Sauce

If you love cilantro, you'll want to put this on everything. It adds flavor and variety to everything from Tofu Scramble (see recipe on p. 29) to Enchiladas (see recipe on p. 120)—and anything in between.

YIELD: 2 cups (474 mL)

- ½ cup (119 mL) water
- ½ cup (8 g) fresh cilantro
- ½ cup (15 g) chopped fresh parsley
- 2 tablespoons white wine vinegar
- 3 cloves garlic
- ⅓ jalapeño pepper, seeded
- ¾ teaspoon sea salt
- ¾ teaspoon freshly ground black pepper
- ½ cup (119 mL) vegetable oil

1. In a blender, place all of the ingredients except the oil and purée the mixture.

2. Once the mixture has been puréed, keep the blender running and through the small cap opening, drizzle in the oil. Keep blending until the sauce is dark green but creamy (it will be very liquidy, but the color should be opaque).

Vegan Worcestershire Sauce

Vegan Worcestershire Sauce is an excellent way to add a hearty, yet sweet, flavor to a variety of dishes—everything from meat substitutes to Logan Bloody Marys (see recipe on p. 53). The downside: traditionally, Worcestershire sauce is made with anchovies, and the vegan store-bought alternatives are expensive. Try making your own with this recipe made from pantry essentials you already have. It will keep for up to 3 months in the refrigerator if well sealed.

YIELD: 2 cups (474 mL)

- 1 cup (237 mL) apple cider vinegar
- ½ cup (119 mL) soy sauce
- ¼ cup (59 mL) water
- ¼ cup (59 mL) blackstrap molasses
- 1 tablespoon organic dark brown sugar
- ½ teaspoon dry ground mustard
- ½ teaspoon onion powder
- ½ teaspoon garlic powder
- ½ teaspoon liquid smoke
- ½ teaspoon ground ginger
- ¼ teaspoon cayenne pepper
- ¼ teaspoon allspice
- ¼ teaspoon ground cloves
- Dash sea salt

1. In a large saucepan over medium-high heat, whisk together all of the ingredients. Bring to a boil.

2. Reduce the heat to low and simmer for 1 minute.

3. Let cool to room temperature and store in an airtight container in the refrigerator for up to 3 months. Shake well before serving.

COOKS' NOTE: If you don't have blackstrap molasses, simply omit it and raise the amount of dark brown sugar to ¼ cup plus 1 tablespoon (75 mL).

Soups and Sandwiches

In this section, we've taken two lunch classics—soups and sandwiches—and put them together. Soups are one of the easiest ways to serve a hearty, heartwarming meal, and our sandwiches helped put us on the map. Together, these are two signatures of our Diner style: comforting and familiar food.

PICTURED: **Delta Po'-Boy (p. 105)**

Soups

While soup can take a long time to prepare, it's really one of the easiest ways to serve up a hearty and heartwarming meal. One-pot meals just make life easier! Make a large quantity on Sunday, when you have time, and package it in individual containers so you and your family can have healthy meals in a hurry throughout the week.

PICTURED: **Squash Bisque (p. 100)**

Basic Vegetable Stock

Vegetable stock takes only moments to make and is a resourceful way to use parts of the vegetables you might otherwise throw away. It will also save you money, because storebought vegetable stock can be pricey.

YIELD: **8–10 cups (1.90–2.36 L)**

- **3 cups (450 g) assorted vegetable stems, stalks, and ends**
- **12 cups (2.80 L) warm water**
- **¼–½ cup (8–16 g) fresh herb stems or sprigs**
- **¼ cup (56 g) nutritional yeast flakes**
- **2 whole cloves garlic or 1 large shallot**
- **2 bay leaves**
- **1 teaspoon whole peppercorns (black or a variety)**
- **1 teaspoon sea salt (or to taste)**

1. In a large stockpot over medium-high heat, combine all of the ingredients. Bring to a boil.

2. Reduce the heat to medium and keep at a gentle boil for 20 to 30 minutes, until all the veggies are extremely tender.

3. Let stand, covered, for 3 to 5 minutes. Strain the stock into a large container. Discard (or snack on) the vegetables.

4. Allow to the stock to cool completely before using. Store the stock in a sealed container in the refrigerator for up to 1 week or in the freezer for up to 2 months.

COOKS' NOTES: Save money by hanging on to the stems, stalks, and rinds of your vegetables after chopping them for a week or so. You can store them in a repurposed produce bag until you accumulate enough to make stock.

Vegetable stock is really best made the day before you need to use it and cooled overnight in the refrigerator.

A Pyrex measuring cup with an airtight lid works perfectly for storing.

TIME SAVER: Vegetable stock isn't just for soup! Use it to add flavor to grains, marinades, and sauces.

Quinoa Chili

Chili is an American staple. The spicy and hearty stew warms from within on a cold autumn or winter night. It's great for feeding your family at fall events like tailgate parties, since chili appeals to almost everyone. It's also perfect to fortify a teenage veggie athlete before a game!

YIELD: 10 cups (2.36 L)

- 2 tablespoons vegetable oil
- 1 cup (150 g) chopped poblano pepper
- 1 cup (150 g) chopped red bell pepper
- 1½ tablespoons chopped chipotle pepper
- 1 cup (150 g) chopped onion
- 1 (15-ounce [425-g]) can dark red kidney beans, rinsed and drained
- ½ cup (120 g) tomato paste
- ¼ cup (8 g) chopped fresh parsley or cilantro
- 2–3 cloves garlic, chopped
- 1 teaspoon sea salt
- ¾ teaspoon freshly ground black pepper
- Dash ground cayenne pepper
- 1 bay leaf
- 8 cups (1.90 L) Basic Vegetable Stock (see recipe on p. 93)
- 1½ cups (356 mL) tomato juice
- 5 cups (925 g) cooked quinoa, for serving
- Sliced avocado, vegan sour cream, and chopped green onion, for topping (optional)

1. In a large stockpot over medium heat, warm the oil. Add the peppers and onion and cook for 7 to 9 minutes, until the onion softens and becomes translucent.

2. Add the beans, tomato paste, parsley, garlic, salt, black pepper, cayenne pepper, and bay leaf to the stockpot. Stir well.

3. Slowly add the Basic Vegetable Stock and tomato juice to the stockpot. Reduce the heat to low and simmer, stirring occasionally, for 30 to 40 minutes, until the chili has thickened. Remove from the heat and allow to cool for 10 minutes. Remove and discard the bay leaf.

4. Line a serving dish with the quinoa and pour the chili over it. Top with the avocado, vegan sour cream, and green onion. Serve immediately.

VARIATION: Add a fiber punch to this recipe by adding 2 cups (1 rinsed and drained can) of black and/or pinto beans.

Curried Cauliflower Soup

This soup is excellent on a winter day. It shows off the comforting "rootyness" of cauliflower that makes the veggie a cold weather staple. The curry powder is just hot enough to warm your core, giving you a revamped feeling on a dreary day.

YIELD: **8–10 cups (1.96–2.36 L)**

- ½ tablespoon vegetable oil
- 1 head cauliflower, chopped
- Sea salt and freshly ground black pepper, to taste
- 1 cup (128 g) chopped carrot
- 1 cup (120 g) chopped celery
- 1 cup (150 g) chopped onion
- 3 cloves garlic, minced
- 2 tablespoons tomato paste
- 1½ tablespoons curry powder
- ½ teaspoon ground turmeric
- ½ teaspoon ground plain paprika
- ½ teaspoon ground cumin
- ½ teaspoon red pepper flakes
- ¼ teaspoon ground nutmeg
- 1 bay leaf
- 2 cups (474 mL) white wine
- 8 cups (1.90 L) Basic Vegetable Stock (see recipe on p. 93)
- 1 (32-ounce [960-mL]) bottle tomato juice
- ½ cup (199 mL) coconut milk
- ¼ cup (56 g) nutritional yeast flakes (optional)
- 2 tablespoons chopped fresh cilantro
- Vegan sour cream and chopped chives, for garnish (optional)

1. In a large sauté pan over medium heat, warm the oil. Add the cauliflower, salt, and black pepper and sauté for 15 minutes, until softened. Remove from the heat and set aside.

2. In a large stockpot over medium heat, combine the carrot, celery, onion, and garlic. Sauté for 8 minutes, until the vegetables are browned and caramelized.

3. Add the tomato paste, curry powder, turmeric, paprika, cumin, red pepper flakes, nutmeg, and bay leaf to the stockpot. Stir well. Cook for 2 to 3 minutes, long enough for the paste to cook off and the spices to become aromatic.

4. Deglaze the stockpot with the wine. Stir well. Cook for another 30 minutes, until the wine has cooked off.

5. Add the Basic Vegetable Stock, tomato juice, coconut milk, and nutritional yeast (if using) to the stockpot. Bring to a boil. Add the cauliflower to the stockpot. Reduce the heat to a simmer. Cook for 10 to 15 minutes. Remove and discard the bay leaf. Reduce the heat to low.

6. Using an immersion blender,* blend the soup until it has a thick, porridge-like texture.

7. Stir in the cilantro. Remove from the heat and let cool for 5 to 10 minutes. Serve garnished with the vegan sour cream and chives.

* It's okay if you don't have an immersion blender. Even if everything is left whole, this soup is still delicious!

VARIATION: You can substitute 1 head cabbage for the cauliflower for an equally delicious cruciferous alternative.

White Bean Bacun Soup

The thick, salty comfort and sweet, yet smoky, flavors of bacun are so indulgent. This is a nice and creamy soup your whole family will love.

YIELD: **8 cups (1.90 L)**

- 1 tablespoon vegetable oil
- 2 cups (300 g) chopped onions
- 2 cups (240 g) chopped celery
- 2 cloves garlic, minced
- ½ jalapeño pepper, finely chopped
- ½ cup (80 g) vegan bacun pieces (see recipe on page 23, or try Lightlife brand)
- 1½ teaspoons sea salt plus more, to taste
- ¾ teaspoon freshly ground black pepper
- 8–10 cups (1.96–2.36 L) Basic Vegetable Stock (see recipe on p. 93)
- 6 cups (908 g) drained and rinsed white beans, divided

1. In a large stockpot over medium heat, warm the oil. Add the onions and celery and sauté for 7 to 9 minutes, until softened and tender.

2. Add the garlic to the stockpot. Cook for 2 minutes.

3. Add the jalapeño pepper to the stockpot. Cook for 3 to 4 more minutes. Stir in the bacun, salt, and black pepper. Cook for 5 to 7 more minutes, until the bacun starts to brown.

4. Add the Basic Vegetable Stock and 4½ cups (681 g) of the beans to the stockpot. Cook for 30 to 45 minutes, until the vegetables are tender.

5. Using an immersion blender,* blend the soup until it is thick but still chunky. Add the remaining 1½ (227 g) cups of beans. Stir well. Cook for 5 to 10 minutes, until warmed through. Add a bit more salt, if needed. Let cool 10 to 15 minutes before serving.

COOKS' NOTE: It's mostly the seeds that make peppers hot, so remove them or leave them in according to your heat preferences. You can also add the jalapeño pepper earlier in the cooking process to reduce the heat a little bit.

* It's okay if you don't have an immersion blender. Even if everything is left whole, this soup is still delicious!

Spicy Potato Soup

Potatoes are comforting, filling, and very inexpensive. Some believe they can help level out your mood. Positive energy and warmth definitely come in handy during our long Chicago winters!

YIELD: **8 cups (1.90 L)**

- 1 tablespoon vegetable oil plus more, if needed
- 2 cups (300 g) chopped yellow onions
- 1 cup (128 g) chopped carrot
- 2 cups (140 g) shredded green cabbage
- 2 cups (300 g) chopped bell peppers
- 6 cups (900 g) diced white potatoes
- 6 cups (1.42 L) Basic Vegetable Stock (see recipe on p. 93)
- 2 teaspoons red pepper flakes
- 1½ teaspoons dried oregano
- 1½ teaspoons dried basil
- 1 bay leaf
- Sea salt, to taste

1. In a large stockpot over medium heat, warm the oil. Add the onions and carrot and sauté for 7 to 9 minutes, until the onions have softened and are translucent.

2. Add the cabbage and bell peppers to the stockpot. Cook for about 8 minutes, until the vegetables are tender.

3. Add the potatoes, Basic Vegetable Stock, red pepper flakes, oregano, basil, bay leaf, and salt to the stockpot. Reduce the heat to low and simmer for 35 to 45 minutes, until the potatoes become soft.* Remove from the heat. Remove and discard the bay leaf. Allow to cool for 5 to 10 minutes before serving.

COOKS' NOTE: You can reduce the amount of red pepper flakes if you think it's too much heat. You can also substitute ½ to 1 fresh hot pepper of your choice for the red pepper flakes if you happen to live in an area that has them in abundance.

* If a knife or fork inserts easily into a piece of potato, the potatoes are done!

Squash Bisque

This apple-tinged Squash Bisque really showcases everything that's plentiful during a Midwestern autumn. Its light flavor will warm you up after a spring rain, too. Whatever lousy weather you're currently facing, this soup will help get you back on track.

YIELD: **8 cups (1.90 L)**

- **2 Granny Smith apples, peeled, cored, and halved**
- **1 medium butternut squash, peeled, seeded, and cut into ½-inch (13-mm) chunks**
- **1 onion, quartered**
- **¼ cup (59 mL) extra virgin olive oil**
- **6 cups (1.42 L) Basic Vegetable Stock (see recipe on p. 93)**
- **4 cups (948 mL) apple juice or cider**
- **3 cloves garlic, minced**
- **3 tablespoons (3 g) fresh or 1 teaspoon dried thyme**
- **Sea salt and freshly ground black pepper, to taste**

1. Preheat the oven to 375°F (190°C).

2. On a baking sheet, combine the apples, squash, and onion. Drizzle them with the oil and roast for 45 minutes, until tender. Be sure to check the vegetables a couple times throughout the roasting process, stirring if necessary. Remove from the oven and allow to cool for 10 minutes.

3. In a blender or the bowl of a food processor fitted with the metal "S" blade, combine the roasted vegetables and fruit with the Basic Vegetable Stock and apple juice and purée until the mixture is completely smooth. You may need to do this in batches to avoid exceeding the liquid fill line of your food processor.

4. Transfer the puréed bisque to a stockpot over medium heat. Add the garlic and thyme and cook for 20 minutes. Season with the salt and black pepper to taste. Serve immediately.

Sandwiches

Of all Chicago Diner specialties, our sandwiches and burgers are the standout favorites. Here's your opportunity to make an authentic Chicago Diner Radical Reuben or Cajun Black Bean Burger in your own kitchen. Come on in—booths are open. Have a seat!

PICTURED: **Bacun Avocado Wrap (p. 114)**

Gluten-Free Black Bean Burgers

Making your own black bean burger at home is easy, rewarding, and fun—not to mention healthier and less costly! This recipe is protein packed with both black beans and the ancient seed quinoa. It has a little kick to it, too, so it's perfect for bringing on the heat!

YIELD: **12 burgers**

- **1 teaspoon vegetable oil**
- **½ cup (75 g) diced onion**
- **½ cup (75 g) diced bell pepper (doesn't matter what color!)**
- **⅓ cup (18 g) sundried tomatoes**
- **2 cloves garlic, chopped**
- **3 tablespoons (45 g) tomato paste**
- **4 cups (688 g) rinsed and drained black beans, divided**
- **⅔ cup (119 mL) water**
- **⅓ cup (28 g) Ener-G Egg Replacer**
- **1 teaspoon ground cumin**
- **1 teaspoon onion powder**
- **1 teaspoon red pepper flakes**
- **1½ cups (278 g) cooked quinoa, divided**
- **Vegan mozzarella, lettuce, tomato, and onion, for garnish**

1. In a large skillet over medium heat, warm the oil. Add the onion, bell pepper, and sundried tomatoes and sauté for 5 to 7 minutes, until the onion and peppers start to soften. Add the garlic and sauté for 2 minutes more, until the onion is translucent and the garlic is browning.

2. Add the tomato paste to the skillet, using a whisk to thin it out.

3. Add 3 cups (516 g) of the black beans and the water, egg replacer, cumin, onion powder, and red pepper flakes to the skillet. Stir or whisk vigorously until everything is combined. Reduce the heat to low and simmer for 10 to 15 minutes, or until the water is absorbed. Remove from the heat.

4. Preheat the oven to 350°F (180°C). Line a baking sheet with parchment paper.

5. Transfer the mixture in the skillet, along with 1¼ cups (231 g) of the quinoa, to the bowl of a food processor fitted with the metal "S" blade and process until the mixture has the consistency of a paste.

6. Transfer the mixture to a large mixing bowl. Using your clean hands, toss the remaining 1 cup (172 g) black beans and the ¼ cup (46 g) quinoa with the paste.

7. Form the mixture into a series of 2-inch (5-cm) balls. Flatten them a bit into patties. Place the patties on the prepared baking sheet.

8. Bake the patties for 15 to 20 minutes. Remove from the oven. Assemble on a platter, garnished with the vegan mozzarella, lettuce, tomato, and onion. Serve warm.

COOKS' NOTE: You can make a bunch of these at once and store them in the refrigerator for 2 weeks or the freezer for up to 3 months. This will come in handy when you get stuck at work late, or have to run to an impromptu cookout.

An ice cream scoop helps keep the size consistent when making burger patties.

Cajun Black Bean Burgers with Creole Remoulade Sauce

This one's for all you vegan hotties out there who need some spice in your life.

YIELD: **6 burgers; 1½ cups (356 mL) Creole Remoulade Sauce**

For the Creole Remoulade Sauce:

- **1 cup (224 g) vegan mayonnaise (Vegenaise)**
- **1 teaspoon Cajun seasoning***
- **¾ teaspoon prepared yellow mustard**

For the Fried Jalapeños:

- **¼–½ cup (59–119 mL) canola oil, for frying**
- **4 whole jalapeño peppers**

For the Sauté Mix:

- **1 teaspoon vegetable oil**
- **¾ cup (113 g) diced onion**
- **1 cup (75 g) sliced mushrooms**
- **2 cloves garlic, minced**
- **3 cups (90 g) fresh baby spinach**

For the Burgers:

- **6 Gluten-Free Black Bean Burger patties (recipe on pg. 102)**
- **6 whole grain buns**
- **1 cup (237 mL) vegan nacho cheese sauce, warmed (we like locally produced Teese)**

To make the Creole Remoulade Sauce:

1. In a small mixing bowl, whisk together all the ingredients and set aside. (Save any leftover sauce in an airtight container; it will remain fresh refrigerated for up to 2 weeks.)

To make the Fried Jalapeños:

1. In a large skillet over medium-high heat, warm the oil until it begins to bubble.

2. Place the whole jalapeño peppers in the skillet and fry for 8 minutes, until they appear slightly wilted. Be sure to move the peppers around frequently to ensure that they cook evenly and to prevent sticking. Remove the skillet from the heat.

3. Remove the jalapeño peppers from the skillet and place them on a plate lined with paper towels. Let them cool for 5 to 7 minutes and then slice them. Set aside.

To make the Sauté Mix:

1. In a large skillet over medium-high heat, warm the oil.

2. Once the oil is warm, add the onion. Cook for 2 minutes. Add the mushrooms and garlic and cook for 5 to 7 minutes, until the onion becomes translucent and the mushrooms are soft.

3. Toss in the spinach and cook for 2 to 4 minutes, until just wilted.

Continued on pg. 104

* Cajun seasoning is a mixture of salt, garlic, onion, paprika, cayenne pepper, oregano, and black pepper that's available in most grocery stores.

Cajun Black Bean Burgers with Creole Remoulade Sauce

(Continued from pg. 103)

To assemble the Burgers:

1. Warm a large skillet over medium heat. Place the patties in the dry skillet for 6 to 8 minutes, long enough to warm them. Remove from the heat. Meanwhile, warm the buns in a toaster or oven on a piece of foil.

2. Transfer the bun bottoms to a serving platter. Place the patties on the bun bottoms and top each with about ⅓ cup (95 g) of the Sauté Mix, 4 to 6 jalapeño pepper slices, 2 tablespoons of the Remoulade Sauce, and 2 to 3 tablespoons of the vegan nacho cheese sauce. Serve immediately.

COOKS' NOTES: Save yourself from doing dishes by making the jalapeño peppers first, discarding most of the oil, and then sautéing the veggie mix in the same pan.

These burgers are particularly delicious with an ice-cold craft brewed beer.

Delta Po'-Boy

This sandwich is an excellent example of how you can save time by making large portions of certain fillings and sides in advance and assembling in different ways throughout the week. This recipe repurposes a couple of other recipes in the book—so let it inspire you to get resourceful and creative with what you find here! By the way, in addition to being inspirational, this sandwich is also enormous and scrumptious.

YIELD: **4 sandwiches**

- 1 cup (70 g) shredded red cabbage
- 1 white onion, sliced
- 1 red bell pepper, julienned
- 2 tablespoons apple cider vinegar
- Sea salt and freshly ground black pepper, to taste
- 2 recipes Blackened Tofu (see recipe on p. 24)
- 2 tomatoes, sliced
- 1 loaf baguette or ciabatta bread, sliced into 8 pieces
- 1½ cups (36 g) julienned romaine lettuce
- 1 cup (237 mL) Creole Remoulade Sauce (see recipe on p. 103)

1. In a large mixing bowl, toss the cabbage, onion, and bell pepper with the vinegar, salt, and black pepper. Set aside.

2. Warm a dry medium skillet over medium heat. Slice the tofu into long strips. Place the tofu in the skillet for 5 to 7 minutes, long enough to warm it through. Remove from the heat.

3. In a medium skillet over medium–low heat, cook the tomato slices for 3 to 5 minutes, until they soften. Remove from the heat.

4. Transfer 4 of the bread slices to a serving platter. Evenly distribute the Blackened Tofu among the slices. Top each with the tomatoes, cabbage slaw, lettuce, and a liberal serving of the Creole Remoulade Sauce. Cover each with the remaining slices of bread. Serve immediately.

VARIATION: You can easily substitute Sea Slaw (see recipe on p. 121) or Sauerkraut (see recipe on p. 86) for the cabbage and pepper slaw in this recipe. Use whatever you have on hand!

Portobello Truffle Melt

A marinade makes these portobellos really tender, and the Truffle Aioli adds a decadent richness to the sandwich. You can use the aioli on all kinds of sandwiches, on veggies, or with pasta.

YIELD: **4 sandwiches**

For the Truffle Aioli:

- **1 cup (224 g) vegan mayonnaise (Vegenaise)**
- **1 tablespoon fresh chopped chives (1 teaspoon dry)**
- **1½ teaspoons white truffle oil**

For the Portobello Truffle Melt:

- **1 loaf baguette or ciabatta bread, sliced into 8 pieces**
- **1 tablespoon extra virgin olive oil**
- **4 cups (908 g) Marinated Portobello Mushrooms (see recipe on p. 26)**
- **1½ cups (336 g) sliced vegan mozzarella cheese (Teese)**
- **1 large tomato, sliced**
- **1 white onion, sliced**
- **2 cups (60 g) arugula**

To make the Truffle Aioli:

1. In a small mixing bowl, whisk together all of the ingredients. Set aside. Store any remaining aioli in an airtight container in the refrigerator for up to 1 week.

To make the Portobello Truffle Melt:

1. Brush the bread lightly with the oil and warm in the oven. Remove from the oven and set aside the slices in stacks of 2 on a serving platter.

2. Place the mushrooms in the empty skillet. Sauté for 7 to 10 minutes, until tender. Remove from the heat.

3. Spread the Truffle Aioli generously on 4 of the bread slices. Divide the mushrooms evenly among the 4 slices coated with the aioli.

4. Atop each pile of mushrooms, layer ¼ of the vegan mozzarella cheese, tomato slices, onion slices, and arugula. Top each sandwich half with the remaining 4 slices of bread.

5. If you have a panini grill, place each sandwich on it for 3 to 5 minutes, until the cheese melts a bit. (If you do not have a panini grill, secure each sandwich with a toothpick and return them, 2 at a time, to the skillet in which you sautéed the mushrooms and heat them for 5 to 7 minutes, until the cheese melts slightly.) Serve immediately.

VARIATION: If you don't have any Vegenaise handy to make the Truffle Aioli, you can drizzle the mushrooms with white truffle oil instead. Fresh parsley can be substituted for the chives, but chives really do add a nice touch. You can also substitute any other kind of mushroom for the portobellos.

Buddha's Karma Burger with Realignment Sauce

Here's an inventive take on a veggie burger. The sweet potato and tofu patty is seasoned deliciously with curry and topped with a mango sauce for a tropical twist. Good karma is sure to follow if you serve this up!

YIELD: **6 Buddha's Karma Burgers; 3 cups (711 mL) Realignment Sauce**

For the Realignment Sauce:

- 2¼ cups (405 g) chopped fresh or frozen and thawed mango
- ¼ cup (59 mL) coconut milk
- ¼ cup (41 g) chopped fresh or frozen and thawed pineapple
- 2½ tablespoons chopped fresh cilantro
- 2½ teaspoons pineapple or orange juice
- ½ teaspoon onion powder
- ½ teaspoon fresh lime juice
- ½ teaspoon ground cayenne pepper
- ½ teaspoon ground cardamom

For the Buddha's Karma Burgers:

- 2 cups (420 g) cooked Mashed Sweet Potatoes (see recipe on p. 143)
- 2 cups (120 g) panko or gluten-free bread crumbs
- 1 cup (150 g) diced onion
- 1 cup (190 g) cooked brown rice
- ½ (12-ounce [341-g]) package extra-firm tofu, drained
- 1 whole clove garlic
- ½ vegetable or vegan chicken flavored bouillon cube
- 2½ tablespoons cornstarch
- ¾ tablespoon curry powder
- ½ tablespoon chopped fresh chives
- ½ tablespoon chopped fresh cilantro
- ½ tablespoon white balsamic vinegar
- 1 teaspoon tomato paste
- ¾ teaspoon ground cumin
- ¾ teaspoon sea salt
- ½ teaspoon ground ginger
- ½ teaspoon ground cayenne pepper
- 6 warmed hamburger buns, for serving
- Chopped cilantro and sliced avocado, for garnish

To make the Sauce:

1. In a blender or the bowl of a food processor fitted with the metal "S" blade, purée all of the ingredients until smooth, but not runny. It should have a mustard-like consistency. Pour into a serving pitcher and set aside.

To make the Buddha's Karma Burgers:

1. Preheat the oven to 350°F (180°C). Line a baking sheet with parchment paper.

2. In a blender or the bowl of a food processor fitted with the metal "S" blade, combine all of the ingredients except the buns and the garnish. Process until the mixture forms a paste-like consistency.

3. Using clean hands, form the batter into ⅔-cup (280-g) balls. Flatten each ball into a patty and place the patties on the prepared baking sheet.

4. Bake for 20 to 25 minutes, turning after 10 minutes to ensure both sides are an even golden brown. Warm the buns in the oven for the last 5 minutes of cooking time. Remove from the oven.

5. On a large serving platter, place the patties on the warmed buns and top with the Realignment Sauce. Garnish with the cilantro and avocado. Serve immediately.

VARIATION: Turn this into a Karmic Salad by crumbling the cooked burgers over greens and tossing the mixture with our Poppyseed Dressing (see recipe on p. 84).

Eggless Salad Wrap

Egg salad is a pretty classic dish. You can use it to stuff a bell pepper, serve it on baguette, or simply spoon it on a bed of lettuce. It's a quick, convenient, versatile, and satisfying staple. Our tofu version is not only totally cruelty free, it's also cholesterol free. The sulfuric taste of black salt really comes in handy when replicating egg dishes, but be careful not to use too much. Black salt's flavor is considerably stronger than that of sea salt.

YIELD: **8 sandwiches**

- 2 (12-ounce [341-g]) packages extra-firm tofu
- ¼ cup (35 g) sunflower seeds
- 1½ cups (336 g) vegan mayonnaise (Vegenaise)
- 1 cup (120 g) diced celery
- ½ cup (15 g) chopped fresh curly parsley
- ½ cup (75 g) sliced green onion
- ¼ cup (33 g) chopped dill pickles
- 3 tablespoons (45mL) prepared yellow mustard
- ¼ teaspoon ground turmeric
- ¼ teaspoon freshly ground black pepper
- ¼ teaspoon black salt or ½ teaspoon sea salt
- 8 whole grain tortillas or bell peppers, for stuffing
- 8 leaves romaine lettuce

1. Unwrap the packages of tofu and place them in a colander or on a plate lined with paper towels to drain for 30 to 60 minutes. Press out any excess moisture.

2. While the tofu is draining, toast the sunflower seeds in a dry skillet over medium heat for 3 minutes, until they turn slightly golden and have a nutty aroma. Remove from the heat. Remove the seeds from the skillet immediately and place them in a large mixing bowl.

3. Add all the remaining ingredients except the tortillas and the romaine to the large mixing bowl. Stir well.

4. Lay the tortillas flat on a clean work surface. Place 1 leaf of romaine and ⅛ of the Eggless Salad on each tortilla.

5. To fold each wrap: Fold over each edge. Use one hand to hold the end of the wrap together and use the other to tightly roll the wrap over on itself. Repeat the process for each wrap. Secure with a toothpick, if necessary. Serve the wraps immediately or wrap them in foil to serve later in the day.

COOKS' NOTES: Be careful to keep the contents pushed toward the center of the wrap, or you'll have trouble rolling it.

Feel free to adjust the specified quantities of vegan mayo and mustard to suit your taste.

VARIATION: You can add 1 cup (110 g) grated carrots or sprouts to the mix and substitute toasted sesame seeds or pepitas for the sunflower seeds.

The Radical Reuben™

The Radical Reuben is our most popular dish. It took home the Vegetarian Times Magazine Readers' Choice Award for Best Recipe in the Midwest in June 2008 and was also featured on TLC's "Best Food Ever: Darn Good Diners" show. Basically, this sandwich rocks, and now you can make it right in your own kitchen!

YIELD: **4 sandwiches**

For the Thousand Island Sauce:

- ¼ cup (56 g) vegan mayonnaise (Vegenaise)
- 3 tablespoons (45 mL) organic ketchup
- 2 tablespoons finely chopped dill pickles

For the Reubens:

- 1 teaspoon vegetable oil
- ½ cup (75 g) sliced yellow onion
- ¼ cup (38 g) sliced red bell pepper
- ¼ cup (38 g) sliced green bell pepper
- 1⅓ cups (303 g) Sauerkraut (see recipe on p. 86)
- 8 slices marble rye bread
- 1 pound (454 g) Seitan Corned "Beef" (see recipe on p. 23)
- 1 cup (112 g) shredded vegan mozzarella cheese (we use Daiya brand for this sandwich)

To make the Sauce:

1. In a small mixing bowl, whisk together all of the ingredients. Set aside.

To make the Reubens:

1. In a large skillet over medium-high heat, warm the oil. Add the onion and peppers and sauté for 7 to 9 minutes, until the onion is translucent. Remove from the heat and transfer the onion and peppers to a medium covered bowl. Set aside.

2. Place the Sauerkraut in the skillet and return it to the heat. Warm it in the skillet for 5 minutes, until it is warmed through. Remove from the heat and transfer the Sauerkraut to a medium bowl. Cover the bowl and set aside.

3. Toast the bread. Place the Seitan Corned "Beef" in the skillet and return it to the heat. Warm it in the skillet for 5 to 7 minutes, until it is warmed through and a little brown on the edges. Remove from the heat and set aside.

4. Place 4 of the toasted bread slices on a serving platter. Divide the Seitan Corned "Beef" evenly among the 4 slices.

5. Atop each pile of Seitan Corned "Beef," layer ¼ of the Sauerkraut, the pepper-onion mix, the vegan mozzarella cheese, and the Thousand Island Sauce. Top each sandwich half with the remaining 4 slices of bread. Slice each sandwich in half and serve immediately.

Tofu Fish Sandwich with Tartar Sauce

This is our vegan answer to a classic fish sandwich. Freezing the tofu gives it a unique texture, and the Tartar Sauce is just a good homemade condiment!

YIELD: **4 sandwiches**

For the Tofu and Marinade:

- 1 (12-ounce [341-g]) package extra-firm tofu, cut into 6 slabs
- 1½ cups (356 mL) vegetable stock
- 2 tablespoons nutritional yeast flakes
- 2 tablespoons garlic powder
- 1 tablespoon onion powder
- 1 tablespoon dried parsley
- 1 teaspoon sea salt
- ½ teaspoon freshly ground black pepper

For the Tartar Sauce:

- 1 cup (224 g) vegan mayonnaise (Vegenaise)
- ⅓ cup (80 g) pickle relish
- 2 tablespoons prepared horseradish
- 1 tablespoon fresh lemon juice
- Sea salt and freshly ground black pepper, to taste

For the Breading:

- 1 cup (60 g) panko breadcrumbs or crushed cornflakes
- ½ teaspoon dried parsley
- ¼ teaspoon sea salt
- Dash freshly ground black pepper
- Dash ground cayenne pepper

For the Sandwich:

- 2–3 tablespoons vegetable oil
- 4 warmed hoagie buns, for serving
- Your favorite variety lettuce, for garnish

To marinate the Tofu:

1. Wrap the individual tofu slabs in plastic wrap and then wrap them again in foil. Freeze for at least 2 days.

2. Thaw the tofu slabs by taking them out of the freezer, removing the foil and plastic wrap, placing them in a shallow dish, and covering them with hot water. Soak the slabs for 10 to 15 minutes.

3. In a small mixing bowl, whisk together all of the Marinade ingredients. Once the Marinade is fully combined, pour it into a shallow dish.

4. Remove each tofu slab from the hot water and wrap it in cheesecloth. Press gently to remove any moisture. The tofu should appear spongy.

5. Place all the tofu slabs in the Marinade and let them sit at room temperature for 30 minutes.

To make the Tartar Sauce:

1. In a small mixing bowl, whisk together all of the ingredients until thoroughly combined. Cover and store in the refrigerator until ready to use.

To make the Breading:

1. In a small mixing bowl, use a fork or whisk to combine all the ingredients. Coat each slab of tofu in the Breading and set aside on a plate.

Continued on pg. 114

Tofu Fish Sandwich with Tartar Sauce *(Continued from pg. 113)*

To make the Sandwiches:

1. In a large, heavy, nonstick skillet over medium-high heat, warm the oil.

2. Place the tofu slabs in the skillet and pan fry for 3 minutes per side, until golden brown. Remove from the heat. Place the tofu slabs on a plate lined with paper towels to absorb some of the excess oil while you prepare the bread.

3. Slice each hoagie bun in half and place them on a serving platter. Spread ¼ of the Tartar Sauce on the bottom half of each bun. Place ¼ of the tofu on each bun. Garnish with the lettuce and serve immediately.

Bacun Avocado Wrap

Wraps are awesome because they take a salad to the next level or scale back an oversized sandwich. They're also very easy to eat on the go. There are countless variations: You could turn almost any of our salads into a wrap, and voila—ready to eat!

YIELD: **6 wraps**

- **6 sundried tomato tortillas**
- **3 ripe avocados, sliced**
- **Juice of ½ lemon**
- **1½ cups (168 g) vegan Cheddar cheese**
- **1½ cups (220 g) diced tomato**
- **1½ cups (235 g) julienned white onion**
- **1 cucumber, sliced**
- **1 (12-ounce [341-g]) package or 24 slices homemade (see recipe on p. 23) vegan bacun**
- **4 cups (144 g) spring mix salad greens**
- **1½ cups (356 mL) Chicago Diner Vegan Ranch Dressing (see recipe on p. 73)**

1. Coat the avocado slices with the lemon juice.

2. Lay the tortillas flat on a clean work surface. Fill the tortillas with ¼ cup each (about 30 g each) of the avocado, vegan cheese, tomato, and onion.

3. Add to each tortilla 3 cucumber slices, 4 bacun strips, ¾ cup (27 g) greens, and 3 tablespoons (45 mL) of the Chicago Diner Vegan Ranch Dressing.

4. To fold each wrap: Fold over each edge. Use one hand to hold the end of the wrap together and use the other to tightly roll the wrap over on itself. Repeat the process for each wrap. Secure with a toothpick, if necessary. Serve the wraps immediately or wrap them in foil to serve later in the day.

COOKS' NOTE: Be careful to keep the contents pushed toward the center of the wrap, or you'll have trouble rolling it.

Entrées

Vegan entrées can range from the complex and time consuming to the simple and quick. This section will teach you how to master the art of veggie dining in your own home. The dishes you'll find here are as visually appealing as they are palate pleasing. Dinner-party guests and family members alike will be astounded by how satisfying and aesthetic a vegan meal can be.

Some of these recipes might look a little complex, but most of them are designed to be made in stages—the components of which you can make in large batches for convenience. In truth, a satisfying vegan dinner can be as simple as a steamed grain, some Blackened Tofu (see recipe on p. 24), and a green vegetable. As you get more comfortable with veggie cooking, you'll simplify and perfect these dishes to fit your own busy lifestyle.

PICTURED: **Enchiladas (Flautas variation) (p. 120)**

Pistachio-Crusted Tofu with Porcini Bread Pudding

This creative dinner was a popular special feature for the Valentine's Day holiday in 2013. The addition of pistachios gives tofu a new twist, and the savory bread pudding is a creative way to save a great day-old salt-top rye or other gourmet bread that might otherwise go to waste. Plate these two alongside your favorite green vegetable, and you'll surely impress your vegan sweetie.

YIELD: **4 entrée servings**

For the Pistachio-Crusted Tofu:

- 1 recipe unbaked Herb-Citrus Tofu (see recipe on p. 20)
- ⅔ cup (102 g) pistachios
- ⅓ cup (50 g) panko
- 1 teaspoon onion powder
- ½ teaspoon granulated garlic
- ½ teaspoon sea salt
- ¼ teaspoon white pepper
- ¾ teaspoon Ener-G Egg Replacer
- 1 tablespoon water
- 1 recipe Lemon Beurre Blanc Sauce (see recipe on p. 119), for topping
- 1 recipe Porcini Bread Pudding, for serving
- Cooked vegetables, for serving

For the Porcini Bread Pudding:

- 4 cups (240 g) cubed day-old bread
- 1½ cups (356 mL) soy milk
- 1–1¼ cups (237–296 mL) vegetable stock
- ¾ cup (168 g) melted vegan margarine
- 3 tablespoons (16 g) Ener-G Egg Replacer
- 2 tablespoons chopped fresh chives
- ½ teaspoon sea salt
- ½ teaspoon freshly ground black pepper
- ½ tablespoon vegetable oil
- ½ yellow onion, diced
- 1½ cups porcini mushrooms (or your favorite kind)
- 2 tablespoons melted vegan margarine, for brushing

To make the Pistachio-Crusted Tofu:

1. Prepare the Herb-Citrus Tofu recipe except the baking step. Slice into 4 slabs. Place on a plate.

2. In the bowl of a food processor fitted with the metal "S" blade, chop the pistachios until they have the consistency of small pebbles. Transfer them to a dry sauté pan over low heat and toast them for 2 minutes. (Keep a close eye on them, as they burn easily.)

3. Preheat the oven to 325°F (160°C). Line 2 baking sheets with parchment paper.

4. Return the toasted pistachios to the bowl of the food processor and and add the panko, onion powder, garlic, salt, and white pepper. Pulse until the mixture has the consistency of a fine breading, but the pistachio pieces remain a little chunky. Transfer the pistachio crusting to a shallow dish.

Continued on pg. 118

Pistachio-Crusted Tofu with Porcini Bread Pudding *(Continued from pg. 117)*

5. In a shallow dish, whisk together the egg replacer and water.

6. Thoroughly coat each piece of the Herb-Citrus Tofu first with the egg replacer mixture and then with the pistachio crusting. Place the crusted tofu slabs on the prepared baking sheets.

7. Bake for 10 to 15 minutes. Remove from the oven.

8. Top the Pistachio-Crusted Tofu with the Lemon Beurre Blanc Sauce and serve with the Porcini Bread Pudding and any cooked vegetable, such as roasted asparagus, Brussels sprouts, or Flashed Greens (see recipe on p. 145).

To make the Porcini Bread Pudding:

1. In a medium mixing bowl, make a sauce for the bread by whisking together the soy milk, vegetable stock, margarine, egg replacer, chives, salt, and black pepper.

2. Place the bread in a large mixing bowl and pour the sauce over it. If the bread remains a little dry, just add a bit more soy milk and stock until the bread is completely moist but not soaked. Set aside.

3. In a large skillet over medium heat, warm the oil. Add the onion and sauté for 5 minutes, until almost tender. Add the mushrooms and sauté for another 5 to 7 minutes, until the mushrooms are tender.

4. Add the sautéed onions and mushrooms to the mixing bowl containing the bread mixture. Using clean hands, carefully fold them together, being extra careful not to break the bread down while mixing. Let the mixture sit at room temperature for 1 hour.

5. Preheat the oven to 325°F (160°C). Lightly grease a 9 × 13-inch (22.5 × 32.5-cm) casserole dish.

6. Add the bread mixture to the prepared casserole dish. Lightly brush the top of the bread mixture with the melted margarine, which will help it turn golden brown.

7. Cover with foil and bake for 20 to 25 minutes. Remove the foil and bake for another 20 to 25 minutes. Remove from the oven. Serve immediately.

Lemon Beurre Blanc Sauce

This sauce is spectacular served over our Pistachio-Crusted Tofu with Porcini Bread Pudding, but it can also be used to brighten up pasta, seasonal veggies, greens, or any tofu dish.

YIELD: **2 cups (474 mL) sauce**

- ¼ cup (59 mL) white wine
- ¼ cup (59 mL) white wine vinegar
- ½ tablespoon fresh lemon juice
- 1 tablespoon finely chopped shallot
- 1 teaspoon lemon zest
- 2 cups melted (474 mL) vegan margarine

1. In a small saucepan over medium-high heat, combine all of the ingredients except the margarine and bring to a boil. Reduce the mixture until it is slightly thickened and has reduced to about ¾ of its original volume. Remove the pan from the heat.

2. Add 1 tablespoon of the margarine to the saucepan and whisk vigorously until it has fully emulsified. Repeat this process, 2 tablespoons to ¼ cup (49 mL) at a time, until the mixture is creamed.

3. Return the saucepan to low heat, and continue to whisk the sauce until the margarine is fully incorporated. Once you've finished the sauce, it should be kept warm, but not too hot, until serving (too much heat will break the sauce). Remove from the heat.

COOKS' NOTES: Make sure the liquid has reduced by at least 25 to 30 percent before adding the margarine. If it hasn't, the sauce will not emulsify.

Be sure to add the margarine slowly. Doing so is essential to emulsification.

If you need to thicken the sauce, add a little flour or nutritional yeast, 1 tablespoon at a time until the desired consistency is reached. Adding 2 to 3 tablespoons of soy creamer could also work.

Enchiladas

Mexican-style dishes are some of the simplest and most satisfying entrées to veganize, and we serve several at our restaurants. One of our most popular entrées is our Flautas, which are basically fried enchiladas (find details on making Flautas in the Variation). Rolling up tortillas and baking them in the oven might be a little easier for veggie dining at home, but we'll leave the choice up to you. Either way, this meal is perfect for a dinner party or a simple family fiesta.

YIELD: **6 Enchiladas; 8 cups (1.90 L) Enchilada Sauce**

For the Enchilada Sauce:

- **3 pounds (1.36 kg) Roma tomatoes**
- **½ cup (50 g) sliced jalapeño peppers (use more or less depending on your spice tolerance)**
- **8–10 whole cloves garlic**
- **¼ cup (59 mL) vegetable oil**
- **1½ cups (225 g) chopped onion**
- **1½ cups (356 mL) vegan sour cream (Tofutti)**
- **1½ teaspoons sea salt**

For the Enchiladas:

- **6 flour tortillas**
- **2 cups (344 g) Spiced Black Beans (see recipe on p. 146) or canned vegan refried black beans**
- **1 cup (210 g) mashed potatoes**
- **1 cup (112 g) vegan Cheddar cheese (Daiya or Teese Nacho)**
- **3 jalapeño peppers, diced**
- **4½ cups (855 g) Mexican Rice (see recipe on p. 142), for serving (optional)**
- **1½ cups (54 g) shredded lettuce, for serving**
- **1½ cups (240 g) diced tomatoes, for serving**
- **1½ cups (356 mL) vegan sour cream, for serving**
- **Avocado slices, for garnish (optional)**

To make the Enchilada Sauce:

1. In a large stockpot over medium-high heat, combine the tomatoes, jalapeño peppers, and garlic and cover with water. Bring to a boil and keep it there for 4 minutes, until the vegetables are tender.

2. Drain and remove the vegetables from the stockpot. Place them in a medium mixing bowl and set aside.

3. In a large skillet over medium heat, warm the oil. Add the onion and sauté for 7 to 10 minutes, until it is golden brown. Remove from the heat and transfer the onion to the mixing bowl.

4. Place the vegetables in the bowl of a food processor fitted with the metal "S" blade. You can also use a hand blender. Process until smooth. Stir in the vegan sour cream and salt. Transfer to a bowl and place, covered, in the refrigerator until ready to use.

To make the Enchiladas:

1. Preheat the oven to 350°F (180°C).

2. Place the tortillas on a clean work surface. Fill each tortilla with 1½ tablespoons black beans, 1 tablespoon mashed potatoes, a sprinkle of the vegan cheese, and a sprinkle of jalapeño pepper. (Be sure to spread the fillings evenly.) Repeat until all the fillings except ½ cup (56 g) of the vegan cheese have been used.

3. Roll up each tortilla and place the Enchiladas seam-side-down in a 9 × 13-inch (22.5 × 32.5-cm) glass baking dish.

VARIATION: To turn this delicious dish into Flautas, omit the black beans, use corn instead of flour tortillas, and skewer 3 to 4 of the filled and rolled Enchiladas per skewer. Fill a large, deep frying pan with 1 to 2 inches (2.5–5 cm) of vegetable oil and bring the oil to a simmer. Pan fry each skewer of Enchiladas for 3 minutes. Plate the Flautas with a scoop of black beans and a scoop of Mexican Rice, and top them with tomato, lettuce, and vegan sour cream.

4. Cover the Enchiladas with 6 cups (1.42 L) of the Enchilada Sauce and the remaining ½ cup (56 g) of the vegan cheese. Bake for 30 minutes, until the Enchiladas are hot and bubbly. Remove from the oven. Serve immediately with sides of the Mexican Rice (if using), lettuce, tomatoes, and vegan sour cream. Garnish with the avocado slices, if using.

Bibimbap

This Korean dish literally translates to "mixed rice" and features a variety of foods in a bowl with rice and a spicy red pepper paste called "gochujang." Our vegan version drops the traditional raw egg and meat and tames the heat of the pepper paste. Gochujang can be hard to find in the States, so you can substitute easier-to-find Sriracha sauce and get similar results. The various add-ins (Asian Red Pepper Sauce, Blackened Tofu, Sea Slaw, and so on) are designed to be made in advance and kept on hand so you can enjoy a scrumptiously spicy veg dinner in a flash.

YIELD: 4 entrée servings

For the Sea Slaw:

- 2 cups (140 g) shredded green cabbage
- 1 cup (70 g) shredded red cabbage
- 1 cup (110 g) shredded carrots
- 1 cup (20 g) arame or any other type of sea kelp, soaked, rinsed, and drained
- ¼ cup (38 g) sliced green onion
- ¼ cup (8 g) chopped fresh parsley
- ⅔ cup (158 mL) rice wine vinegar or apple cider vinegar
- ½ cup (119 mL) sesame oil
- ¼ cup (59 mL) mirin
- 2 tablespoons fresh lemon juice
- 1 teaspoon freshly ground black pepper
- Dash sea salt

For the Asian Red Pepper Sauce:

- ½ cup (119 mL) + 2 tablespoons white wine vinegar
- ½ cup (119 mL) + 2 tablespoons water
- ½ cup (119 mL) sesame oil
- ¼ cup (59 mL) Gochujang paste (or Sriracha sauce)
- ¼ cup (50 g) organic granulated cane sugar
- 2 tablespoons tamari
- 2 tablespoons sesame seeds

Continued on pg. 122

Bibimbap *(Continued from pg. 121)*

For the Bok Choy–Broccoli Stir-Fry:

- **1 tablespoon sesame oil**
- **2 cups (176 g) broccoli florets**
- **4 cloves garlic, minced**
- **2 cups (340 g) cored and sliced (1-inch [2.5-cm] pieces) bok choy**
- **2 tablespoons soy sauce**
- **Juice of ¼ lemon**
- **1 tablespoon grated fresh ginger**

For the Serving Bowls:

- **4 cups (760 g) cooked rice**
- **2 cups (496 g) Blackened Tofu (see recipe on p. 24), Hickory Tempeh Strips (see recipe on p. 21), or Korean-Style Seitan (see Variation below)**
- **1 sliced cucumber, for garnish**
- **1 cup (128 g) shredded carrots, for garnish**

To make the Sea Slaw:

1. In a large mixing bowl, combine the cabbages, carrots, arame, green onion, and parsley.

2. In a small mixing bowl, whisk together the rice wine vinegar, sesame oil, mirin, lemon juice, black pepper, and salt, making a dressing.

3. Pour the dressing over the vegetables and toss until coated. Cover the bowl and refrigerate overnight.

To make the Asian Red Pepper Sauce:

1. In a large mixing bowl, combine all of the ingredients. Use an immersion blender (optimally fitted with a whisk attachment) or whisk to blend the sauce until it is smooth and even. Set aside.

For the Bok Choy–Broccoli Stir-Fry:

1. In a large skillet over medium heat, warm the oil. Add the broccoli and garlic and sauté for 3 minutes, stirring often and adding splashes of water to prevent sticking.

2. Add the bok choy, soy sauce, lemon juice, and ginger to the skillet. Stir and sauté for 5 minutes, until the bok choy ends are slightly wilted. Remove from the heat.

To prepare the Serving Bowls:

1. Prepare 4 3-cup (711-mL) bowls for serving. Place a ½-cup (95-g) scoop of rice and a ½-cup (124-g) portion of the Blackened Tofu, side by side, in each bowl.

2. Transfer ½ cup (65 g) of the Bok Choy–Broccoli Stir-Fry to each of the serving bowls, next to the rice.

3. Transfer ½ cup (35 g) of the Sea Slaw to each of the serving bowls, next to the Blackened Tofu. Garnish with the cucumber and carrots. Serve each bowl with ½ cup (59 mL) of the Asian Red Pepper Sauce.

TIME SAVER: Make the Asian Red Pepper Sauce in advance, perhaps even at the same time you make the Sea Slaw (i.e., the day before you plan to serve the Bibimbap). Use whatever protein, salad, and greens you have in your fridge instead of what's called for in the recipe.

VARIATIONS: Feel free to substitute shiitake mushrooms for the broccoli. You can also throw in 1 cup (104 g) bean sprouts.

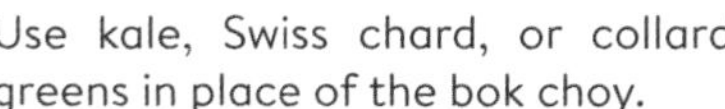

Use kale, Swiss chard, or collard greens in place of the bok choy.

Substitute Sauerkraut (see recipe on p. 86), Overnight Pickles (see recipe on p. 147) or kimchee for the Sea Slaw.

To make an accompanying seitan, simply sauté 1 pound (454 g) of seitan chunks or strips in ½ cup (119 mL) Asian Red Pepper Sauce over medium heat for 5 to 7 minutes.

Jamaican Jerk Kabobs

Caribbean food isn't really about heat alone—it's about creating a distinct and heavily spiced flavor array. Nothing exemplifies that more than Jamaican Jerk Sauce. These skewers are perfect for a summer barbeque, especially if you want to bring the vegan heat.

YIELD: 6 skewers

For the Jamaican Jerk Sauce:

- 2 scotch bonnet (habañero) peppers
- 1 small leek or 1 bunch scallions, chopped
- 1 (4–ounce [114-g]) jar pimentos
- 5 cloves garlic
- Juice of 2 limes
- ¼ cup (59 mL) + 1 tablespoon molasses
- 3 tablespoons (45 mL) canola oil
- 2 tablespoons fresh thyme
- 2 tablespoons soy sauce
- 2 tablespoons organic ketchup
- 1 tablespoon sesame oil
- 1 teaspoon freshly ground black pepper
- 1 teaspoon ground nutmeg
- ¼ heaping teaspoon ground cinnamon
- ¼ teaspoon ground ginger

For the Jamaican Jerk Kabobs:

- 1 (12-ounce [431-g]) package extra-firm tofu
- 1 potato, cut into 1½-inch (4-cm) cubes
- 1 bell pepper, cut into 1½-inch (4-cm) cubes
- 1 small red onion, cut into 1½-inch (4-cm) cubes
- 12 small whole mushrooms
- 6 bamboo skewers
- 3–4 cups (570–760 g) cooked brown rice, for serving

Continued on pg. 126

Jamaican Jerk Kabobs *(Continued from pg. 125)*

To make the Jamaican Jerk Sauce:

1. In the bowl of a food processor fitted with the metal "S" blade, purée all of the sauce ingredients. Transfer to a large mixing bowl and set aside.

To make the Jamaican Jerk Kabobs:

1. Unwrap the package of tofu and place it on a plate lined with paper towels to drain for 1 hour.

2. Slice the tofu into 1½-inch (4-cm) cubes.

3. Using clean hands, alternate cubes of the tofu, potato, bell pepper, and onion, as well as the whole mushrooms, onto the 6 skewers.

4. Place the skewers in a 9 × 13-inch (22.5 × 32.5-cm) casserole dish and cover with all but ¼ cup (59 mL) of the Jamaican Jerk Sauce. Place in the refrigerator and marinate for 8 hours or overnight.

5. Set the oven to broil.

6. Broil the Jamaican Jerk Kabobs in the casserole dish for 15 minutes, turning and brushing the Kabobs with the remaining ¼ cup (59 mL) Jamaican Jerk Sauce after 7 minutes. Remove from the oven. Serve individually plated over the brown rice.

COOKS' NOTES: These kabobs are also delicious grilled.

Feel free to mix up the veggies with whatever you have available—pineapple would also be nice!

Spinach Turnovers

This classic and versatile dish can be served as large triangles, entrée style, or as small triangles to make a delicious appetizer. Serve with Tzatziki Sauce (recipe follows), Tahini Dressing (see recipe on p. 71), or even our Lemon Beurre Blanc Sauce (see recipe on p. 119).

YIELD: **4 entrée servings**

- **2 tablespoons extra virgin olive oil**
- **½ onion, thinly sliced**
- **2 small cloves garlic, chopped**
- **3 pounds (1.36 kg) baby spinach leaves, washed and dried**
- **2 tablespoons fresh lemon juice**
- **2 tablespoons roughly chopped fresh mint**
- **Pinch sea salt**
- **Freshly ground black pepper, to taste**
- **1 (16-ounce [454-g]) package phyllo dough**
- **2 cups (474 mL) melted vegan margarine, for brushing**
- **1½ cups (356 mL) Tzatziki Sauce, for serving**

1. In a large skillet over medium heat, warm the oil. Add the onion and cook for 7 to 9 minutes, until the onion softens and becomes translucent.

2. Next, add the garlic and cook for 30 seconds. Reduce the heat to medium-low and add the spinach. Toss the spinach in the hot pan for 2 or 3 minutes, until it starts to wilt. Remove from the heat and stir for an additional 2 minutes, until all the spinach has wilted.

3. In a medium mixing bowl, combine the onion-spinach mixture, lemon juice, mint, salt, and black pepper. Toss until the filling is well combined. Set aside.

4. Preheat the oven to 375°F (190°C). Line a baking sheet with parchment paper.

5. On a clean work surface, lay out 1 sheet of phyllo dough from the package's stack and brush with the margarine. Place another sheet of phyllo dough on top of the first one and brush it with the margarine. Repeat 2 more times.

6. Once you have 4 brushed sheets on top of one another, slice the stack into 4 equal-width strips (note that the width of the strips will determine the final size of your turnovers).

7. Using a spatula, spread ¼ of the filling on the bottom right side of one of the rectangles. Fold the bottom left corner up and over the filling so that the bottom edge is even with the right side. Continue folding up and over until you form a triangle. Brush the outside of the triangle with the margarine. Place the turnover on the prepared baking sheet. Repeat for each of the 4 turnovers.

8. Bake for 20 minutes, until golden brown. Remove from the oven. Cool slightly on a wire rack and serve immediately with the Tzatziki Sauce.

Tzatziki Sauce

Tzatziki is a Greek cucumber yogurt sauce that's always great for topping pita sandwiches or kabobs. It goes really well with Mediterranean dishes like spinach turnovers, but you can also use it as a salad dressing, dipping sauce, or even a sandwich spread.

YIELD: 1½ cups (356 mL)

- ½ cup (112 g) vegan mayonnaise (Vegenaise)
- ¼ cup (59 mL) + 3 tablespoons (45 mL) vegan sour cream
- 1½ tablespoons soy milk
- 2 teaspoons chopped fresh dill (optional)
- 1½ teaspoons red wine vinegar
- ¾ teaspoon fresh lime juice
- ½ cucumber, peeled, seeded, and diced
- ¼ white onion, minced
- 1 clove garlic, minced

1. In a medium mixing bowl, combine the vegan mayonnaise, vegan sour cream, soy milk, dill (if using), vinegar, and lime juice. Mix together until the sauce is fully combined and creamy.

2. Fold the cucumber, onion, and garlic into the mixture. Serve immediately or store in an airtight container in the refrigerator for 5 days.

VARIATION: Pair the Tzatziki Sauce with the Italian-Style Seitan (see recipe on p. 22) and you've got the makings for our Vegan Gyros. All you need to add is pita bread with chopped lettuce, tomato, and onion for toppings.

Moussaka

This Greek-style lasagna casserole is one of Jo's very best dishes. It's a great option for a hearty whole-plant food entrée. It uses eggplant slices in lieu of pasta, rendering this version gluten free!

YIELD: **6 entrée servings**

For the Filling:

- 2 tablespoons olive oil
- 1 medium onion, chopped
- 2 cups (150 g) sliced mushrooms
- ½ cup (57 g) coarsely chopped walnuts
- 1 tablespoon gluten-free soy sauce
- 3 Roma tomatoes, diced
- 1 (15-ounce [425-g]) can cannellini beans, drained and rinsed
- 1–2 cinnamon sticks
- 4 cloves garlic, minced
- ½ teaspoon sea salt
- ¼ teaspoon freshly ground black pepper
- ⅓ cup (10 g) chopped fresh parsley
- ½ teaspoon ground cinnamon

For the Sauce:

- ½ cup (119 mL) vegetable oil
- ½ cup (79 g) rice flour
- 4 cups (948 mL) unsweetened almond milk
- 2 tablespoons nutritional yeast flakes
- ½ teaspoon sea salt
- ¼ teaspoon ground nutmeg
- Dash freshly ground black pepper

For the Eggplant Layers:

- 2 medium eggplants, sliced into ½-inch- (13-mm-) thick circles
- 1½ teaspoons sea salt
- 1 cup (237 mL) almond milk
- 1 cup (158 g) rice flour
- ¼ cup (40 g) cornmeal
- 1 tablespoon dried oregano
- ½ teaspoon freshly ground black pepper
- 3 tablespoons (45 mL) extra virgin olive oil, for brushing
- 2–3 tablespoons nutritional yeast flakes, for sprinkling

To make the Filling:

1. In a large skillet over medium heat, warm the oil. Add the onion and sauté for 7 minutes, until almost translucent.

2. Add the mushrooms, walnuts, and soy sauce to the skillet. Stir and sauté for 5 to 7 minutes, until the onion is translucent and the mushrooms begin to cook down.

3. Add the tomatoes, beans, cinnamon sticks, garlic, salt, and black pepper to the skillet, stir, and cook for 10 minutes.

4. Add the fresh parsley and ground cinnamon to the skillet. Stir. Remove from the heat, cover, and set aside.

To make the Sauce:

1. In a large skillet over medium heat, warm the oil. Once the oil is hot, whisk in the flour. Cook for 2 to 3 minutes, until you can smell the flour cooking.

2. Slowly add the almond milk and nutritional yeast to the skillet, stirring constantly to prevent lumps. Reduce the heat to medium-low and cook for 10 minutes, until the sauce reaches a thick, gravy-like consistency.

3. Add the salt, nutmeg, and black pepper to the skillet. Stir well. Remove from the heat, cover, and set aside.

To make the Eggplant Layers:

1. In a large mixing bowl, place the eggplant slices. Cover with water. Add the salt and soak for 30 minutes.

2. Preheat the oven to 350°F (180°C). Line a baking sheet with parchment paper.

3. Drain and rinse the eggplant slices. Place them on a plate lined with paper towels and pat dry.

4. In a medium shallow bowl, place the almond milk. In another medium shallow bowl, mix together the flour, cornmeal, oregano, and black pepper.

5. Dip each eggplant slice in the almond milk, and then in the flour mixture. Place the slices on the prepared baking sheet.

6. Bake for 35 minutes, until golden brown, flipping halfway through the baking time and brushing well with the oil to help them brown. Remove from the oven and set aside to cool slightly.

7. When they are cool enough to handle, place ½ of the eggplant slices in the bottom of a 9 × 13-inch (22.5 × 32.5-cm) glass baking dish.

8. Remove the cinnamon sticks from the Filling and spread the Filling evenly over the first eggplant layer. Top with the remaining eggplant slices and pour the Sauce over the top.

9. Sprinkle the top of casserole lightly with the nutritional yeast and bake for 30 to 45 minutes, until bubbly. Remove from the oven. Let stand 5 minutes. Serve.

COOKS' NOTE: Be sure not to finely grind or chop the walnuts; they must be coarsely chopped.

VARIATIONS: You could also make this recipe with thin slices of zucchini cut longways instead of the eggplant.

To transform the recipe into Eggplant Napoleon, layer the eggplant with Tofu Ricotta (see recipe on p. 25) instead of the Filling found here.

Use 1 cup crumbled tempeh instead of mushrooms and walnuts, if you prefer. You can also use white or navy beans instead of cannellini, if that's what you happen have in your pantry.

Truffled Portobello Mushrooms with Potato–Daikon Pancakes and Creamed Leeks

This Valentine's Day special is a wonderful dish to serve for a small dinner party, or you can scale back the recipe a bit and make it for a romantic evening in with your honey. Pair with a nice glass of wine and your favorite green vegetable. It's helpful to make the Potato–Daikon Pancakes in advance to save on prep time.

YIELD: **6 entrée servings**

For the Truffled Portobello Mushrooms:

- 2 pounds (908 g) Marinated Portobello Mushrooms (see recipe on p. 26)
- White truffle oil, for drizzling

For the Creamed Leeks:

- 2 teaspoons vegetable oil
- 4 large leeks, thinly sliced
- 2 tablespoons gluten-free flour mix (Bob's Red Mill or Trader Joe's brands are great)
- 1 cup (237 mL) vegetable stock (or 1 cup [237 mL] water and ½ vegetable bouillon cube)
- 1 cup (237 mL) almond milk
- 2 tablespoons nutritional yeast flakes
- ½ teaspoon sea salt
- ½ teaspoon freshly ground black pepper

For the Potato–Daikon Pancakes:

- 1 pound (454 g) russet potatoes, peeled and shredded
- ½ pound (227 g) daikon radishes, peeled and shredded
- ¼ cup (17 g) gluten-free flour mix (Bob's Red Mill or Trader Joe's brands are great)
- 1 teaspoon sea salt
- ½ teaspoon freshly ground black pepper
- ½ teaspoon baking powder
- ½ tablespoon vegetable oil
- ¼ cup (38 g) sliced green onions, for garnish
- White truffle oil, for drizzling (optional)
- Cooked green vegetables, for serving

To make the Truffled Portobello Mushrooms:

1. In a large mixing bowl, lightly drizzle the Marinated Portobello Mushrooms with the truffle oil. Set aside.

To make the Creamed Leeks:

1. In a large skillet over medium heat, warm the oil. Add the leeks and sauté for 5 minutes, until golden and tender.

2. Add the flour to the skillet, stirring constantly, and cook for 1 to 2 minutes.

3. Gradually add the vegetable stock to the skillet, whisking constantly. Cook, stirring occasionally, for 10 to 15 minutes, until the sauce reduces by half.

4. Gradually add the almond milk and then the nutritional yeast to the skillet, whisking constantly to prevent lumps. Take care not to add the milk too quickly, or you could break the roux.

Continued on pg. 134

Truffled Portobello Mushrooms with Potato–Daikon Pancakes and Creamed Leeks *(Continued from pg. 133)*

5. Add the salt and black pepper to the skillet. Reduce the heat to low and simmer for 8 minutes, until the sauce reaches a gravy-like consistency. Remove from the heat and set aside.

To make the Potato–Daikon Pancakes:

1. Place the potatoes and radishes in a colander lined with paper towels and squeeze as much moisture as possible from the vegetables. Replace the towels 1 to 2 times and repeat the squeezing process if necessary in order to get the maximum amount of moisture out of them.

2. In a large mixing bowl, combine the potatoes, radishes, flour, salt, black pepper, and baking powder and mix them well with your clean hands.

3. On a clean work surface, form the mixture into 6 ¼-cup (116-g) balls and flatten them a bit into pancakes. Place them on a plate.

4. In a large skillet over medium heat, warm the oil. Add 3 of the pancakes to the skillet and fry for 5 minutes on the first side and 3 to 4 minutes on the other side, until golden brown.

5. Place 6 shallow entrée-sized bowls on the counter. Ladle ¼ cup of the Creamed Leeks in the bottom of each bowl. Place 1 of the Pancakes on top of each serving of the Creamed Leeks and top with ⅙ of the Truffled Portobello Mushrooms mixture.

6. Lightly garnish with the green onions and drizzle each bowl with the truffle oil, if using. Serve immediately with a side of cooked green vegetable of your choice, such as steamed asparagus, Flashed Greens (see recipe on p. 145), Brussels sprouts, or even a green salad.

COOKS' NOTES: Be sure to clean the leeks well and use both the white and green parts, as you would with green onions.

You can add more nutritional yeast or flour to the Creamed Leeks if you need to thicken it up a bit. Add 1 tablespoon at a time until desired consistency is reached. Conversely, add more stock or almond milk if you need to thin it out a bit.

Truffle oil is incredibly delicious and has a very strong flavor. A little goes a very long way. Try using a ⅛ teaspoon measure until you get the hang of it. Never cook with truffle oil; instead, drizzle it lightly after the meal is cooked. It has a very low burn temperature and will ruin your dish if heated too much.

VARIATION: If you can't find daikon radishes, simply make the recipe with 1½ pounds (681 g) potatoes instead.

Roasted Veggie Polenta with Red Pepper Sauce

Polenta is extremely easy to make, but it impresses people every time. Whip up a whole pan on a day when you have more time in your kitchen, and use it all week long. It freezes well, too.

YIELD: **6 entrée servings**

For the Polenta:

- 6 cups (1.42 L) vegetable stock
- 2 cups (484 g) yellow corn grits
- 3 tablespoons (45 mL) canola oil
- 1 tablespoon dried parsley
- ½ teaspoon granulated garlic
- 1 cup chiffonaded basil, for garnish

For the Red Pepper Sauce:

- 1 (28-ounce [793-g]) can roasted red peppers, drained
- ¼ cup (60 g) tomato paste
- 3 cloves garlic
- ½ cup (12 g) fresh basil, chopped
- Sea salt and freshly ground black pepper, to taste

For the Roasted Veggies:

- 2 tablespoons balsamic vinegar
- ½ teaspoon dried Italian herbs
- 1 teaspoon sea salt
- Freshly ground black pepper, to taste
- 8–10 cups (1.20–1.50 kg) chopped or sliced assorted vegetables (zucchini, yellow squash, portobellos, eggplant, and carrots)

To make the Polenta:

1. In a large stockpot over high heat, bring the vegetable stock to a boil.

2. Gradually stir the grits into the stock. Whisk the mixture thoroughly to eliminate any clumps. Reduce the heat to medium–low and simmer for 35 minutes, stirring often with a long-handled spoon (as the mixture tends to bubble and pop). Scrape the bottom and sides of the stockpot often, as grits tend to stick and burn quite easily. The mixture should become very thick, as if a spoon could stand on its own.

3. Add the oil, parsley, and garlic to the stockpot and stir well. Simmer for 5 more minutes. The Polenta should be very thick. Remove from the heat.

4. Lightly grease a 9 × 13-inch (22.5 × 32.5-cm) baking dish. Pour and then press the Polenta into the dish, smoothing it over with a spoon or rubber spatula.. Cool uncovered at room temperature for 30 minutes. Cover and refrigerate overnight.

Continued on pg. 137

Roasted Veggie Polenta with Red Pepper Sauce (Continued from pg. 135)

To make the Red Pepper Sauce:

1. In the bowl of a food processor fitted with the metal "S" blade or using an immersion blender, purée the red peppers, tomato paste, and garlic.

2. In a large stockpot over medium-low heat, simmer the red pepper mixture for 15 minutes, until reduced by half.

3. Add the basil, salt, and black pepper to the stockpot. Stir well and remove from heat. Set aside.

To make the Roasted Veggies:

1. Preheat the oven to 375°F (190°C).

2. In a large mixing bowl, whisk together the vinegar, herbs, salt, and black pepper.

3. Toss the vegetables with the vinegar mixture. Place the vegetables on a baking sheet and roast them for 30 to 40 minutes, depending on which vegetables you choose. Check after 20 minutes or so and stir as necessary to ensure even roasting. Remove from the oven and set aside.

To assemble the dish:

1. During the last 25 minutes of the Roasted Veggies roasting time, place the refrigerated Polenta in the oven to warm it.

2. Place 6 shallow entrée-sized bowls on the counter. Cover the bottom of each bowl with the Red Pepper Sauce. Slice the Polenta into 6 squares and, using a spatula, place 1 square on top of the Sauce in each bowl. Cover the Polenta with liberal stacks of the Roasted Veggies. Garnish with the basil.

COOKS' NOTES: Making your own vegetable stock is an easy way to use veggie scraps you would otherwise toss or compost. In a pinch, you can substitute 6 cups (1.42 L) water and 2 vegetable bouillon cubes for the stock in this recipe.

Once the Polenta has set, you can cut it with a round cookie cutter or glass to make circles instead of squares.

You can use a regular blender if you don't have a food processor. The consistency may not be as smooth, but it will still taste great.

VARIATION: Consider adding a heaping scoop of Tofu Ricotta (see recipe on p. 25) between the Polenta and Roasted Veggies.

Pasta Carbonara

Pasta Carbonara is a rich, decadent dish that's steeped in tradition. The sweet notes in this dish's sun-dried tomato cream sauce complement the smokiness of the vegan bacun perfectly. This is sure to satisfy everyone at your dinner table.

YIELD: **6 entrée servings**

- **16 ounces (454 g) dried pasta, any shape**
- **1 teaspoon extra virgin olive oil**
- **½–1 tablespoon vegetable oil**
- **1 (12-ounce [341-g]) package (18 strips) vegan bacun (try the Lightlife brand, or homemade [page 23])**
- **¼ cup (56 g) + 2 tablespoons vegan margarine (we like Earth Balance)**
- **¼ cup (121 g) + 2 tablespoons unbleached organic all-purpose flour**
- **4 cups (948 L) vegetable stock**
- **¾ cup (42 g) chopped sun-dried tomatoes**
- **2 tablespoons soy milk**
- **1½–2 teaspoons red pepper flakes**
- **Sea salt and freshly ground black pepper, to taste**
- **2 cups (268 g) chopped (½-inch [13-mm] pieces) fresh asparagus**
- **1¼ cups (181 g) green peas**
- **¼ cup (14 g) chopped sun-dried tomatoes, for garnish**
- **¼ cup (8 g) chopped fresh parsley, for garnish**

1. In a large stockpot over medium heat, cook the pasta according to package directions. Remove from the heat, drain, and rinse with cold water. Toss with the olive oil to prevent sticking. Return the pasta to the stockpot and set aside.

2. In a large skillet over medium heat, warm the vegetable oil. Add the bacun and pan fry it for 2 to 4 minutes, until browned. Remove from the heat. Once the bacun is cool enough to handle, chop it into bits and transfer it to a small bowl. Set aside.

3. In a large, heavy saucepan over medium heat, melt the margarine. Add the flour and cook for 3 minutes, stirring well to avoid clumps.

4. Slowly add the vegetable stock to the saucepan, stirring constantly. Reduce the heat to low and let simmer, uncovered, for 20 minutes.

5. Add the ¾ cup sundried tomatoes, soy milk, red pepper flakes, salt, and black pepper. Remove from the heat. Using an immersion blender (or transfer to a regular blender), purée until smooth and creamy.

6. Return to the heat (and, if using a regular blender to purée, the saucepan). Add the asparagus and peas to the saucepan and simmer for 10 minutes, until the sauce takes on the thickness and consistency of spaghetti sauce. Remove from the heat.

7. Transfer the sauce to the stockpot containing the pasta and toss well. You may need to restore to medium-low heat to thicken the sauce and really coat the noodles. The sauce should not be runny.

8. Place 6 shallow entrée-sized bowls on the counter. Place 2 cups (76 g) of the pasta in each bowl. Garnish with the remaining sundried tomatoes and parsley.

COOKS' NOTES: Carbonara is traditionally served with spaghetti noodles, but you can use any kind of pasta you like. It works very nicely with campanelle or farfalle, for example.

If you're having trouble getting the sauce to thicken, add some nutritional yeast, 1 tablespoon at a time. Nutritional yeast helps sauces become creamier and conveys a cheesy richness.

VARIATION: You can easily make this dish gluten free by using your favorite gluten-free dried pasta, substituting rice flour for the all-purpose flour, and substituting chopped, toasted walnuts for the seitan bacun.

Fettuccine with Cashew Alfredo

Deciding to forgo dairy and butter doesn't mean never having another hankering for a rich, creamy Alfredo sauce. Raw cashews soaked in water do a great job of simulating the creaminess of rich dairy. Nuts are a good source of protein without the cholesterol a traditional dairy Alfredo sauce would contain.

YIELD: **6 entrée servings**

- 1 cup (138 g) raw cashews
- 12 ounces (341 g) vegan fettuccine pasta
- 6–8 cups (180–240 g) baby spinach
- 1 tablespoon extra virgin olive oil
- 1 cup (237 mL) almond milk, divided
- ¼ cup (56 g) + 1 tablespoon nutritional yeast flakes
- 2 tablespoons fresh lemon juice
- 6 whole cloves garlic
- 1 tablespoon dried onion
- 2 teaspoons canola oil
- 1½ teaspoons sea salt or more, to taste
- 1½ teaspoons dried parsley
- Dash dry ground mustard (finely ground)
- Freshly ground black pepper, to taste
- 2 tablespoons chopped fresh parsley, for garnish

1. In a small mixing bowl, cover the cashews with water and let soak 30 minutes to 1 hour.

2. In a large stockpot, cook the pasta according to package directions, making sure to add the spinach to the cooking water 2 minutes before the cooking time is over. The spinach should wilt immediately. Remove from the heat and drain. Return the pasta and spinach to the stockpot. While the pasta is cooling, add the olive oil and toss lightly. Set aside.

3. In the bowl of a food processor fitted with the metal "S" blade or a blender, combine the cashews and their soaking water, ¼ cup (59 mL) of the almond milk, and the nutritional yeast, lemon juice, garlic, dried onion, canola oil, salt, dried parsley, mustard, and black pepper. Process until the cashews form a smooth, creamy liquid, stopping to scrape the sides of the bowl at least twice.

4. Transfer the mixture to a large saucepan over medium-low heat. Whisk in the remaining almond milk and cook for 5 to 7 minutes, whisking constantly. Remove from the heat. Add more salt if needed.

5. Once the sauce has reached the consistency of a rich gravy, pour it over the pasta and spinach in the stockpot and toss well. Transfer to a large serving bowl, garnish with the fresh parsley.

VARIATION: Consider adding vegan "scallops" or "shrimp" to this recipe. For example, you can prepare 1 package of Sophie's Vegan Breaded Scallops according to the package directions and serve it on a bed of the Fettuccine with Cashew Alfredo.

Vegetables and Other Side Dishes

In this section, you will discover how to prepare side dishes that work well as an accompaniment to a wide range of foods. Greens, grains, and potatoes can be used as entrée sides; as fillings in quesadillas, enchiladas, scrambles, and sandwiches; or simply joined together as an all-side-item meal.

PICTURED: **Brussels Sprouts with Garlic and Lemon (p. 148)**

Mexican Rice

This is the type of dish you'll want to make in large batches and use in a variety of ways throughout the week. Over the years, we've incorporated Mexican Rice into a wide variety of dishes—everything from Mexicana Brunch Bowls to the Chipotle Firehouse Wrap. This is an excellent grain dish that can bulk up any meal.

YIELD: **4 cups (760 g)**

- 2 cups (380 g) uncooked brown rice
- 4 cups (948 mL) vegetable stock
- 1 cup (160 g) diced tomatoes
- ¼ cup (32 g) diced carrots
- ¼ cup (38 g) diced potatoes
- ¼ cup (35 g) fresh or frozen green peas
- ¼ cup (40 g) fresh or frozen corn
- ¼ cup (38 g) diced onion
- 3 tablespoons (45 mL) tomato juice
- 2 cloves garlic, minced
- 1 teaspoon sea salt

1. In a large stockpot, prepare the rice according to package directions, using the vegetable stock instead of water. Cook for 30 minutes, or until about ⅔ of the stock has been absorbed by the rice.

2. Add the remaining ingredients. Cover the stockpot, reduce the heat to low, and cook for another 20 to 30 minutes, until all the liquid has been absorbed. Keep a close eye on the pot to make sure it does not dry out. Transfer to a serving bowl and serve immediately.

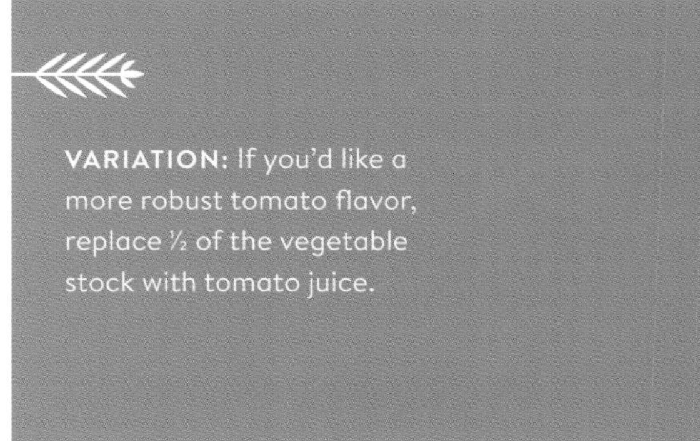

VARIATION: If you'd like a more robust tomato flavor, replace ½ of the vegetable stock with tomato juice.

Mashed Sweet Potatoes

Not only are sweet potatoes scrumptious, they're also packed with beta carotene and Vitamin A. This root vegetable can be prepared in a variety of ways, but we think you'll really enjoy this simple version. Mashed Sweet Potatoes work well as a side dish or also as a filling for quesadillas. Keep a little on hand for those nights when you get stuck at work or at your kids' soccer game.

YIELD: **2 cups (420 g)**

- 1 pound (454 g) whole sweet potatoes
- 1½ tablespoons melted vegan margarine or extra virgin olive oil
- ½ teaspoon organic granulated cane sugar
- ¼ teaspoon ground cinnamon
- Sea salt and freshly ground black pepper, to taste

1. Preheat the oven to 350°F (180°C). Line a baking sheet with parchment paper.

2. Wash the potatoes thoroughly. Pierce them 2 or 3 times with a fork, wrap them in foil, and place them on the prepared baking sheet. Bake them for 1 hour, until an inserted fork glides through easily. Remove from the oven and set aside to cool completely.

3. Using an ice cream scoop or large spoon, separate the potato flesh from the skin. Discard the skins. Transfer the flesh to a large mixing bowl.

4. Add the margarine to the mixing bowl. Using a hand mixer, heavy whisk, or potato masher, mash the potatoes and margarine together until smooth.

5. Add the remaining ingredients and stir until just combined. Transfer to a serving bowl and serve immediately.

VARIATIONS: For a lower-glycemic version of Mashed Sweet Potatoes, omit the sugar.

Add 2 tablespoons to ¼ cup (56 g) nutritional yeast flakes to amp up the richness of this dish.

Flashed Greens

Dark, leafy greens seem to have boundless health benefits. Kale is a powerhouse of nutrients—particularly Vitamins K, A, and C; fiber; and antioxidants with anti-cancer benefits. It's better to cook greens quickly by flash sautéing them. Cooking them all the way down or boiling diminishes their nutritional content. Remove the kale stems, which are bitter and tough to eat.

YIELD: **6 servings**

- 1 tablespoon vegetable oil
- 3 cloves garlic, minced
- 1 tablespoon minced fresh ginger
- 1 pound (454 g) kale
- 1 pound (454 g) baby spinach
- 1–2 tablespoons water
- Sea salt and freshly ground black pepper, to taste

1. In a large skillet over medium heat, warm the oil. As soon as the oil becomes hot, add the garlic and ginger and stir.

2. Immediately add the kale to prevent the garlic and ginger from burning. Stir well and sauté for 2 to 3 minutes. Add the spinach and stir for 1 to 2 more minutes.

3. Add the water and remove from the heat. Add the salt and pepper and stir. Set aside, covered, for 1 to 2 minutes. Transfer to a serving bowl and serve immediately.

COOKS' NOTE: Pull the kale from the stalk with your hands and massage the greens to to reduce bitterness and increase tenderness. You can save the stems and sauté them in a separate skillet with ½ cup (75 g) chopped onion for 7 to 9 minutes, until the onion is translucent, to bulk up your greens.

VARIATIONS: Brighten up this recipe by sprinkling the finished dish with 1 tablespoon fresh lemon juice and/or ½ tablespoon red pepper flakes.

Use any kind of greens in this recipe. It's fun to substitute mustard greens or rainbow chard for the kale.

Try tossing in ¼ cup (56 g) nutritional yeast flakes to turn these into cheesy-style greens.

Spiced Black Beans

This is our version of refried black beans. You really can't go wrong with these. Use them with Sweet Potato Quesadillas (see recipe on p. 48) or Enchiladas (see recipe on p. 120), or as a base for a Mexican-style pizza or tacos. They are super easy to make and are a yummy snack or filler to have in your fridge.

YIELD: **4 cups (544 g)**

- **1¼ cups (215 g) dried black beans, rinsed and drained**
- **4–6 cups (948mL–1.42 L) vegetable stock or 4–6 cups (948mL–1.42 L) water + 1 vegetable bouillon cube**
- **1 tablespoon red wine vinegar**
- **1¼ teaspoons garlic powder**
- **1¼ teaspoons onion powder**
- **1¼ teaspoons ground cumin**
- **½ teaspoon sea salt**
- **½ teaspoon red pepper flakes**
- **¼ teaspoon fresh lemon juice (juice of 1 lemon wedge)**

1. In a large saucepan over medium heat, place the beans, cover with the vegetable stock, and bring to a boil. Reduce the heat to low, cover, and simmer for 1 hour, until the beans are soft. (You may need to add some water during the cooking time if the liquid cooks off before the beans soften, so be sure to check the liquid level every 15 minutes or so.) Remove from the heat.

2. Drain, reserving any remaining cooking liquid. Transfer to the bowl of a food processor fitted with the metal "S" blade and allow them to sit for 30 minutes, until cool enough to handle.

3. Add all of the remaining ingredients to the food processor bowl and process until smooth, yet slightly chunky. (Be careful not to over-process.) Serve.

COOKS' NOTE: Reserve some of the vegetable stock used to cook the beans and add it in just before you blend to help smooth out the beans, if necessary.

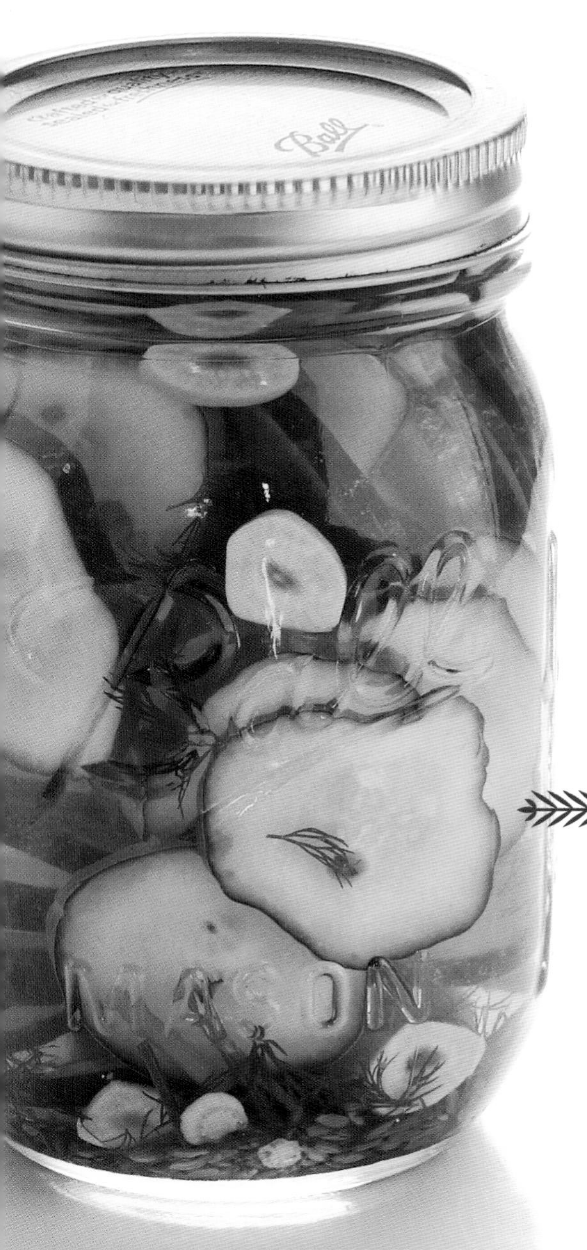

Overnight Pickles

If you've always wanted to pickle but find canning intimidating, then fear not! This is a quick and simple pickling method that even the most novice cook can master.

YIELD: **4 cups (572 g)**

- **2 cups (474 mL) cold water**
- **½ cup (119 mL) white vinegar**
- **1 bunch fresh dill weed, chopped**
- **3 cloves garlic, sliced**
- **2 tablespoons organic granulated cane sugar**
- **½ tablespoon sea salt**
- **1 teaspoon cumin seed**
- **Dash ground cayenne pepper**
- **4 cups (520 g) sliced pickling cucumbers**

1. In a medium saucepan over medium-low heat, combine the water, vinegar, dill, garlic, sugar, salt, cumin, and cayenne pepper. Bring to a simmer and cook for 5 minutes. Remove from the heat and set aside.

2. In a large mixing bowl, combine the cucumbers and the brine. Cover, refrigerate overnight, and voilà! Pickles! Serve immediately or store in an airtight jar or container for up to 1 to 2 weeks.

VARIATION: Try mixing this pickling recipe up with different seasonal veggies. It's also really good for mushrooms, carrots, cauliflower, and bell peppers.

Brussels Sprouts with Garlic and Lemon

This recipe is a perfect example of keeping it simple. All the ingredients are basics you should always have in your kitchen. Change out the Brussels sprouts for broccoli or asparagus, if that's what you have or if that's what's on sale this week!

YIELD: 4 (½-cup [44-g]) servings

- Cooking spray, for greasing
- 2 tablespoons extra virgin olive oil
- 1½ tablespoons chopped fresh parsley
- 1 tablespoon fresh lemon juice
- 3 teaspoons minced garlic
- ½ teaspoon sea salt
- Dash onion powder
- 1 pound (454 g) Brussels sprouts, halved
- Freshly ground black pepper, to taste

1. Preheat the oven to 400°F (200°C). Lightly grease a baking sheet with the cooking spray.

2. In a large mixing bowl, whisk together the oil, parsley, lemon juice, garlic, salt, and onion powder.

3. Add the Brussels sprouts to the bowl and mix thoroughly, until all the Brussels sprouts are well coated in the mixture. Add the black pepper and stir again.

4. Transfer the Brussels sprouts to the prepared baking sheet and bake for 12 to 15 minutes, or a little longer if you want them to be less crunchy. You'll know they're about done when the edges start to brown. Remove from the oven, place in a serving bowl, and serve.

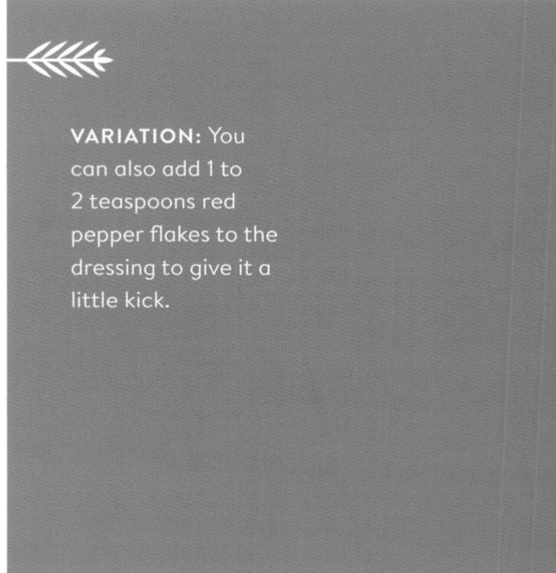

VARIATION: You can also add 1 to 2 teaspoons red pepper flakes to the dressing to give it a little kick.

Spaghetti Squash

Spaghetti squash is one of the easiest and most visually appealing side dishes you can make. You can even toss the stringy cooked squash with marinara sauce to make gluten-free "pasta."

YIELD: **4–6 servings**

- **1 medium spaghetti squash, halved**
- **½ tablespoon extra virgin olive oil**
- **1 tablespoon Fresh Herb Mix (recipe follows) or 1 teaspoon herbes de Provence**
- **Sea salt and freshly ground black pepper, to taste**

1. Scoop the seeds out of the center of the squash.*

2. Preheat the oven to 350°F (180°C).

3. Place the squash halves, flat sides down, in a 9 × 13-inch (22.5 × 32.5-cm) baking dish filled with 1 inch (2.5 cm) of warm water.

4. Steam in the oven for 1 hour. Let sit for 5 minutes, until cool enough to handle, then scoop out the insides and place in a large mixing bowl. Toss with the olive oil, Fresh Herb Mix, salt, and black pepper. Serve.

* Consider reserving the seeds and roasting them for a tasty snack later. To roast the seeds, place them in a mixing bowl and toss them lightly with ½ tablespoon olive oil, ½ teaspoon sea salt, a healthy dash of cayenne pepper, and a dash of freshly ground black pepper. Bake on a lightly greased baking sheet for 12 minutes at 375°F (190°C), until golden brown.

Fresh Herb Mix

This is a fabulous mix of all the great herbs that are seasonally available in the Chicago area! The mix is great to use in any vegetable dish or tossed with olive oil and vinegar for a salad dressing. Swap out these herbs with what you can find in your local farmers' market.

YIELD: **1 cup (25 g)**

- **½ cup (15 g) finely chopped fresh parsley**
- **3 tablespoons finely chopped fresh basil**
- **1 tablespoon fresh oregano leaves**
- **2 teaspoons fresh thyme leaves**

1. In a small mixing bowl, combine all of the ingredients. For the oregano and thyme, rub the leaves a bit with your fingertips to help break them down. Mix well. Use immediately or refrigerate in an airtight container for 1 to 3 days.

Desserts

For many, baking seems to be among the most intimidating of the vegan culinary arts. Let's face it: Baking in general seems to frighten away the faint-of-kitchen-heart, but fear not! Baking is just a series of simple science experiments. The main trick with vegan baking is figuring out what to substitute for eggs in any given recipe. Once you get that down, it's really quite easy.

PICTURED: **Strawberry Rhubarb Pie (p. 163)**

EGG REPLACERS AND FAT SUBSTITUTES

While vegan baked goods are always cholesterol free (because they don't contain animal-derived products), they aren't necessarily low fat. There are, however, some great ways to cut the fat and still make sure your cookies, breads, or cakes remain moist. Following are some of our favorite changeups for oil or eggs in vegan recipes.

PURÉED PRUNES: Use ⅓ cup (58 g) of them if a recipe calls for ½ cup (119 mL) of oil. They work particularly well in chocolate-flavored baked goods—especially cookies.

RIPE BANANAS: Half of a mashed banana can be a great substitute for 1 egg. It's excellent in muffins, certain cakes, and sweetened breads.

SOY YOGURT: Instead of an egg, try using ¼ cup (57 g) nondairy yogurt. It's a great option in sweetened breads and dense cakes.

MILLED FLAXSEED: Milled flaxseed and water is a great failsafe egg substitution that works in pretty much any type of recipe—including those in which the egg is present simply to bind ingredients together. Flaxseed's mega punch of Omega-3 fatty acids is an added bonus! Mix 1 tablespoon milled flaxseed with 3 tablespoons (45 mL) water to equal 1 egg.

SILKEN TOFU: Use ¼ cup blended silken tofu in place of 1 egg. This is the right choice for dense muffins, pound cakes, or other types of dense cakes.

ENER-G EGG REPLACER: 1½ teaspoons Ener-G + 2 tablespoons water equals 1 egg. Like silken tofu, it's a great choice for moist cakes and pound cakes, but it's also great for biscuits. Ener-G makes baked goods rise perhaps even a little too much, so keep that in mind when experimenting with it. Ener-G also works really well for binding and keeping breading intact.

Cocoa Mousse Cake

Fluffy, moist chocolate cake layered between a rich, whipped chocolate mousse ... this cake will send you to pure vegan bliss. It's nearly impossible to stop yourself from polishing off a whole slice in seconds.

YIELD: **1 (8-inch [20-cm]) cake**

For the Cocoa Mousse:

- **2 cups (320 g) dairy-free semisweet chocolate chips**
- **1 cup (237 mL) soy milk**
- **1 tablespoon brown rice syrup**
- **6 ounces (170 g) silken tofu, drained**

For the Cake:

- **2¼ cups (281 g) whole wheat pastry flour or unbleached organic all-purpose flour**
- **½ cup (43 g) cocoa powder**
- **¾ teaspoon baking soda**
- **¾ teaspoon baking powder**
- **½ teaspoon sea salt**
- **1¾ cups (415 mL) brown rice syrup**
- **1 cup (237 mL) water**
- **¼ cup (59 mL) + 1 tablespoon vegetable oil**
- **1 teaspoon pure vanilla extract**
- **1 teaspoon white vinegar**
- **Fresh berries, mint sprigs, or orange zest, for topping (optional)**

To make the Cocoa Mousse:

1. Place the chocolate chips in a double boiler over low heat and allow it to melt, stirring constantly. If you don't have a double boiler, you can place a small saucepan inside another saucepan with about 1 inch (2.5 cm) of simmering water in it. When using this method, be sure that you do not let the bottom of the upper saucepan touch the water (it will burn the chocolate), and that you do not let any water get into the upper saucepan (it will break the chocolate, i.e., cause it to separate).

2. In a blender, combine the soy milk, brown rice syrup, and tofu and purée the mixture. Add the melted chocolate chips to the blender and blend until smooth. Transfer to a bowl and chill in the refrigerator for 1 hour.

To bake the Cake:

1. Preheat the oven to 350°F (180°C; 325°F [160°C] for convection ovens). Lightly grease the bottom and sides of an 8-inch cake pan.

2. In the bowl of a stand mixer fitted with the paddle attachment, sift together the flour, cocoa powder, baking soda, baking powder, and salt on low speed until well combined.

3. In a medium mixing bowl, combine the brown rice syrup, water, oil, vanilla extract, and vinegar.

4. Pour the wet ingredients into the bowl of the stand mixer. Mix well on low speed for 2 to 3 minutes, until fully combined and smooth. Be sure to scrape the sides of the bowl to make sure all the dry ingredients are thoroughly mixed. Pour the cake batter into the prepared cake pan.

5. Bake for 30 minutes, until a cake tester inserted into the center comes out clean. Remove from the oven.

6. Let the cake cool in the pan on a wire rack for 30 minutes. Carefully invert the pan onto a cake plate to remove the cake. (You may need to slide a knife along the edge of the pan before flipping if you're afraid the cake might stick.)

7. Once the cake is completely cool, frost it with the Cocoa Mousse. A warm cake will melt frosting, and if you don't wait, your cake will be glazed rather than frosted. Top with the fresh berries, mint sprigs, or orange zest, if using. Serve immediately or store in an airtight container in the refrigerator for 5 to 7 days.

BAKERS' NOTES: You can substitute maple syrup, agave nectar, or any other natural liquid sweetener for the brown rice syrup.

If you don't have a sifter, you can always use a mesh strainer instead. It's actually faster and just as effective.

TIME SAVER: Make extra Cocoa Mousse and serve it in a parfait glass for a kid-friendly dessert in a flash. The Cocoa Mousse will stay fresh stored in an airtight container in the refrigerator for 7 days.

VARIATIONS: If the idea of a Chocolate–Peanut Butter Cake appeals to you, use our Peanut Butter Frosting (see the Variation recipe on p. 155) in place of the Cocoa Mousse.

To make the flavor of this cake a little more interesting, add ½ teaspoon orange or mint extract to the mousse at the same time you add the soy milk.

To turn this into a layer cake, double both the Cocoa Mousse and Cake recipes and add a layer of Cocoa Mousse between the 2 cakes.

Yellow Birthday Cake

If you've ever wondered what to make for a dairy-free kiddo's birthday party, here is your answer! This is our yellow cake recipe, which can be frosted with whatever you prefer and decorated for your special occasion.

YIELD: **1 (8-inch [20-cm]) double-layer cake**

- **Cooking spray, for greasing**
- **2¼ cups (272 g) unbleached organic all-purpose flour**
- **⅔ cup (84 g) whole wheat pastry flour**
- **1 teaspoon sea salt**
- **1 teaspoon baking soda**
- **1 teaspoon baking powder**
- **2 cups (400 g) organic granulated cane sugar**
- **½ cup (102 g) vegetable shortening**
- **½ cup (119 mL) vegetable oil**
- **1½ tablespoons pure vanilla extract**
- **2¼ cups (635 mL) soy milk**
- **1 recipe Chicago Diner Vanilla Frosting (recipe follows)**

1. Preheat the oven to 350°F (180°C). Lightly spray the bottom and sides of 2 8-inch (20-cm) cake pans with the cooking spray.

2. In a large mixing bowl, sift together the flours, salt, baking soda, and baking powder. Set aside.

3. In the bowl of a stand mixer fitted with the paddle attachment, combine the sugar and shortening. Cream the mixture on medium-low speed for 2 to 4 minutes, until it reaches a sandy texture.

4. Add the oil and vanilla extract to the bowl of the stand mixer. Mix well on low speed for 3 minutes, until stiff peaks form in the mixture.

5. As the mixer runs on low speed, slowly add the dry ingredients and soy milk to the bowl of the mixer in thirds, alternating as you go along. Mix until thoroughly combined, stopping to scrape down the sides of the bowl periodically. Pour the cake batter into the prepared cake pans.

6. Bake for 60 minutes, until golden brown and cake testers inserted into the center come out clean. Remove from the oven.

7. Let the cake cool in the pan on a wire rack for 20 minutes. Carefully invert the pan onto a cake plate to remove the cake. (You may need to slide a knife along the edge of the pan before flipping if you're afraid the cake might stick.)

8. Once the cake is completely cool, frost it with the Chicago Diner Vanilla Frosting. A warm cake will melt frosting, and if you don't wait, your cake will be glazed rather than frosted. Serve immediately or store in an airtight container in the refrigerator for 5 to 7 days.

Chicago Diner Vanilla Frosting

This is our light and creamy vegan frosting. It's fantastic, but not overly sweet. This recipe has been used at the Diner for years and is based on an original recipe by Chef Jo's grandma, Gladys.

YIELD: **4 cups (1.06 kg)**

- **1 cup (237 mL) soy milk**
- **½ cup (61 g) unbleached organic all-purpose flour**
- **1½ cups (306 g) vegetable shortening**
- **1⅔ cups (334 g) organic granulated cane sugar**
- **2 cups (448 g) vegan margarine**
- **2 tablespoons pure vanilla extract**

1. In a small saucepan over medium heat, cook the soy milk and flour for 5 to 10 minutes, whisking constantly to prevent burning and sticking, until the mixture is thick and paste-like. Remove from the heat. If the mixture is not smooth, puree it with a hand blender.

2. Transfer the flour paste to a large mixing bowl. Cover and let cool completely at room temperature.

3. In the bowl of a stand mixer fitted with the paddle attachment, combine the shortening and sugar. Cream the mixture on medium-low speed for 5 to 10 minutes, until it reaches a fluffy texture. Add the margarine and mix until combined.

4. Add the cooled flour paste and vanilla extract to the bowl of the stand mixer. Increase the speed to high and mix for 5 minutes, until the frosting is light and fluffy. Use immediately or store in an airtight container in the refrigerator for up to 1 month.

VARIATIONS: You can turn this into Chocolate Frosting by adding 3 tablespoons (16 g) sifted cocoa powder to the bowl of the stand mixer when you blend in the flour paste.

To make our incredibly delicious Peanut Butter Frosting, add ½ cup (129 g) + 2 tablespoons natural peanut butter to the bowl of the stand mixer when you blend in the flour paste. To make Chocolate-Peanut Butter Frosting, also add 3 tablespoons (16 g) sifted cocoa powder at the same time.

Chocolate Ganache

Chocolate Ganache adds a scrumptious and decadent flair to everything from fresh fruit to cheesecakes to a chocolate peanut butter shake. The best part is that you can make this recipe in a flash. Try it—you'll love it!

YIELD: **1 cup (237 mL)**

- **1½ cups (240 g) dairy-free semisweet chocolate chips**
- **½–⅔ cup (119–158 mL) soy milk**
- **1 teaspoon vegan margarine**

1. Place the chocolate chips in a shallow metal mixing bowl. Set aside.

2. In a small saucepan over medium heat, heat the soy milk. Once the soy milk becomes warm, reduce the heat to low and cook for 5 minutes, until scalding. Bubbles should form around the edges. Remove from the heat.

3. Pour the hot soy milk over the chocolate chips. Add the margarine and let stand for 1 minute. Stir together until smooth. Pour the Chocolate Ganache over any of your favorite desserts or store in a squeeze bottle or sealed Mason jar in the refrigerator for up to 1 week.

TIME SAVER: Make Chocolate Ganache in advance and keep it on hand in a squeeze bottle. When you're ready to use the Chocolate Ganache, submerge the bottle in a hot water bath for 5 minutes, which will return it from a solid to a viscous liquid.

Raw Chocolate Mousse

Chocolate (or its primary ingredient, cacao) is now recognized for its antioxidant properties. If you're trying to satisfy your urge for a rich, creamy, and chocolatey dessert without completely negating your healthy eating habits, raw cacao desserts are a perfect option. This recipe provides a chocolate fix in a hurry. You'll have all the health benefits of avocados and cacao in one fabulous and simple raw dish.

YIELD: **6 (½-cup [202-g]) servings**

- **3 ripe avocados**
- **¾ cup (65 g) cacao powder**
- **¼ cup (59 mL) agave nectar**
- **1 teaspoon pure vanilla extract**
- **½ teaspoon ground cinnamon**
- **Fresh or frozen berries, for topping**

1. In a blender, combine all of the ingredients except the berries. Blend on high for 2 to 3 minutes. (If you don't have a blender, you can use a whisk.)

2. Pour into serving bowls and serve immediately, topped with the berries.

Raw Orange–Ginger Cheezecake

Raw desserts are an inventive way to combine healthy ingredients and satisfy your sweet tooth, all at the same time. You won't be able to stop eating this decadent, citrus-infused treat.

YIELD: **1-2 (8-inch [20-cm]) cheezecakes**

For the Crust:

- **1¼ cups (140 g) almond or flax meal**
- **½ cup (50 g) raw pecans, walnuts, or macadamia nuts**
- **½ cup (40 g) raw unsweetened coconut flakes**
- **¾ cup (110 g) pitted medjool dates**
- **¼ teaspoon sea salt**
- **2 tablespoons agave nectar (optional; if the dates are very soft, you may not need it)**

For the Filling:

- **4½–5 cups (621–690 g) raw cashews**
- **1½ cups (356 mL) agave nectar**
- **2 cups (474 mL) + 2 tablespoons freshly squeezed orange juice**
- **Juice of 1 lemon or 3 limes**
- **1½–2 tablespoons fresh grated ginger**
- **1 teaspoon sea salt**
- **1½ cups (356 mL) coconut oil, melted**
- **1 teaspoon orange zest**

To make the Crust:

1. In the bowl of a food processor fitted with the metal "S" blade, combine all of the ingredients except the maple syrup. Pulse until the mixture is coarse and crumbly, but sticking together a bit. If needed to bind the mixture, add the maple syrup and continue to pulse until just combined. Be careful not to overprocess the mixture.

2. Using clean hands, press the crust mixture into 8-inch (20-cm) pie plates or a lightly greased (with coconut oil) 8-inch (20-cm) springform pan. Spread the crust mixture evenly and very firmly across the bottom of the pan. If you are using pie plates, you will probably have enough crust mixture for 2 pies, depending on the depth of the plates. Set aside.

To make the Filling:

1. Soak the cashews in warm water for 3 hours, draining and re-covering with warm water about halfway through the process. At the end of the soaking time, the cashews should be plump and pliable. Drain.

2. In the bowl of a food processor fitted with the metal "S" blade, purée the cashews with the agave nectar, orange juice, lemon juice, ginger, and salt until the mixture is smooth and no large pieces of the cashews remain. Add the melted coconut oil and purée until fully combined.

To make the Cheezecakes:

1. Pour the mixture into the prepared pan or plates and freeze overnight.

2. Allow the Cheezecakes to thaw slightly at room temperature for 30 minutes before slicing. Sprinkle the orange zest over the Cheezecakes. Serve.

BAKERS' NOTE: You can make your own almond meal by finely grinding almonds in a food processor fitted with the metal "S" blade, or you can find store-bought versions at any health food store. To make flax meal, grind whole flaxseeds in a coffee grinder or blender. Never try to grind flaxseeds in a food processor!

TIME SAVER: Make a double batch of the crust and store it in the refrigerator (for 3 weeks) or freezer (for up to 3 months) for next time.

VARIATIONS: If you don't like the flavor or texture of coconut, or simply can't find unsweetened coconut, substitute 1 cup (100 g) of any variety of chopped raw nuts.

To make a plain Cheezecake, use lemon or lime juice instead of the orange juice and omit the ginger. You can change up the juices in many ways depending on what you have and what flavor you're going for.

Chicago Diner Vegan Cheezecake with Granola or Chocolate Cookie Crust

To many skeptics, the idea of a vegan cheesecake sounds like an oxymoron. Our talented vegan bakers have devised a miraculously satisfying cheesecake recipe that's absolutely perfect in texture. This recipe proves that you can actually have your vegan cheesecake and eat it too!

YIELD: **1 (6-inch [15-cm]) cheezecake**

For the Granola Crust:

- **Cooking spray, for greasing**
- 1¼ **cups (113 g) quick-cooking oats**
- 6½ **teaspoons pure maple syrup, divided**
- 1½ **tablespoons brown rice syrup**
- ¼ **cup (59 mL) melted vegan margarine**

Or for the Chocolate Cookie Crust:

- ⅔ **cup (66 g) vegan chocolate cookie crumbs**
- 2 **tablespoons organic granulated cane sugar**
- 2 **teaspoons sifted cocoa powder**
- 1 **tablespoon melted vegan margarine**
- 1 **teaspoon soy milk**

For the Filling:

- 1 **pound (454 g) vegan cream cheese (Tofutti)**
- 1 **(12-ounce [341-g]) package silken tofu, drained for about 30 minutes**
- ¾ **cup (178 mL) vegetable oil**
- ¾ **cup (150 g) organic granulated cane sugar**
- 2 **tablespoons cornstarch**
- 1 **tablespoon + 1 teaspoon pure vanilla extract**
- 2½ **teaspoons fresh lemon juice**
- ¼–½ **teaspoon sea salt (depending on the saltiness of your particular brand of cream cheese)**
- ¼ **teaspoon ground cardamom**
- **Fresh berries or Chocolate Ganache (see recipe on p. 156), for topping**

To make the Granola Crust:

1. Preheat the oven to 350°F (180°C). Lightly grease a 9 × 9-inch (22.5 × 22.5-cm) baking dish and a 6-inch springform pan with the cooking spray.

2. Make the granola by stirring together the oats, 2 teaspoons of the maple syrup, and the brown rice syrup. Transfer the mixture to the prepared baking dish.

3. Bake for 10 to 12 minutes, until golden brown. Remove from the oven and allow to cool completely.

4. In the bowl of a food processor fitted with the metal "S" blade, pulse the granola until it becomes very fine and no large chunks remain.

5. Add the melted margarine and remaining maple syrup to the bowl of the food processor and process until just combined.

6. Using clean hands, press the crust mixture into the prepared springform pan. Spread the crust mixture evenly and very firmly across the bottom of the pan. Bake for 12 minutes and then set aside until the Filling is ready.

Continued on pg. 160

Chicago Diner Vegan Cheezecake with Granola or Chocolate Cookie Crust *(Continued from pg. 159)*

Or to make the Chocolate Cookie Crust:

1. Lightly spray a 6-inch (15-cm) springform pan with the cooking spray.

2. In a medium mixing bowl, stir together the cookie crumbs, sugar, and cocoa powder.

3. Add the melted margarine and soy milk to the mixing bowl and stir until fully combined.

4. Using clean hands, press the crust mixture into the prepared springform pan. Spread the crust mixture evenly and very firmly across the bottom of the pan. Bake for 12 minutes and then set aside until the Filling is ready.

To make the Filling:

1. Preheat the oven to 300°F (150°C).

2. In the bowl of a food processor fitted with the metal "S" blade or a blender, combine all of the ingredients except the fresh berries or Chocolate Ganache and process until smooth. Pour the Filling over the prepared Crust.

3. Bake for 1 hour 20 minutes. Raise the temperature to 350°F (180°C) and bake an additional 5 to 10 minutes, until the top becomes lightly golden. Remove from the oven.

4. Let the Cheezecake cool at room temperature until it is cool to the touch and has partially set up. Refrigerate overnight so it can set up completely. Serve topped with fresh berries or Chocolate Ganache.

BAKERS' NOTE: If you like, you can make either crust and partially bake it for later use in a pie. To do so, bake the crust only at 350°F (180°C) for 10 to 12 minutes.

VARIATIONS: To make a Chocolate Chip Cheezecake, fold ¼ cup (75 g) dairy-free semisweet chocolate chips into the Filling after it has been processed.

To make a Fruit Coulis Cheezecake, combine ½ cup (75 g) of any chopped fresh fruit, a splash of agave nectar or maple syrup, ¼ teaspoon lemon extract, ⅛ teaspoon pure vanilla extract, and a bit of citrus zest in a saucepan over medium heat and reduce the mixture for 10 minutes, until a thick syrup forms. (The Fruit Coulis will be ready when it thoroughly coats the back of a spoon dipped into the pan.) Allow the Coulis to cool completely and swirl it into the Cheezecake Filling after you transfer it into the prepared Crust.

Homemade Pie Crust

Pies are quite possibly the most intimidating of all the homemade pastries in the American repertoire. Telling friends that you've baked a pie will likely impress them. Little do they know that it can be as easy as, well, pie. Rolling out the crust is the challenging part, but after one or two trial runs, you'll have the hang of it for sure.

YIELD: **1 (8-inch [20-cm]) double-crust pie**

- **1 cup (125 g) whole wheat pastry flour**
- **1 cup (121 g) unbleached organic all-purpose flour**
- **1 teaspoon sea salt**
- **1 teaspoon baking powder**
- **⅔ cup (139 g) palm oil shortening**
- **⅓–½ cup (79–119 mL) ice water**
- **6–8 cups (1.53–2.04 kg) pie filling of your choice**

1. In a medium mixing bowl, sift together the flours, salt, and baking powder. If you don't have the patience for sifting, you can simply use a whisk or fork to blend them together.

2. Using a pastry blender or fork, cut the shortening into the flour mixture until the dough takes on a pebble-like form.

3. Make a well in the center of the dough. Slowly add ⅓ cup (79 mL) ice water and with clean hands, mix the dough together until it forms a ball. Add more water, if needed, until dough just holds together. (The amount of water needed can vary based on humidity levels in your kitchen.)

4. Preheat the oven to 350°F (180°C). Lightly grease an 8-inch (20-cm) pie plate.

5. Shape the dough into a ball and divide it in half.

6. Transfer the dough balls to a clean, lightly floured work surface or pastry mat. Roll each half of the dough out into a 10-inch (25-cm) round shape with a ⅛-inch (3-mm) thickness. (Getting the dough to spread evenly is the toughest part. You must also try to keep it as round as possible. If one edge juts out too far into an oval shape, your crust will be thicker in that area.)

7. To transfer the bottom crust to your prepared pie plate, curl it slightly over the rolling pin. Center it over the pie plate and drape it over.

8. Fill the bottom crust with your choice of pie filling.

9. Fold the excess dough over the edge of the pie plate. If making a single-crust pie, pinch the edge with your fingers or gently press it together with a fork to create a more attractive border.

10. For a two-crust pie, follow the same process to transfer the top crust to the pie. Drape it carefully over the pie. Pinch the edges of the top crust into the edges of the bottom crust to seal it, or use a fork. Slice 3 holes in the center of the top crust to vent while baking.

11. Bake for 20 minutes, depending on the needs of the filling you have selected for the pie. Remove from the oven and allow to cool for 1 hour. Slice and serve.

BAKERS' NOTES: If you don't have a sifter, you can always use a mesh strainer instead. It's actually faster and just as effective.

"Cutting in" is a baking term used to describe the adding of a solid fat to a flour or dry mixture. Using a food processor fitted with the metal "S" blade makes cutting in the shortening quite fast and easy.

You can make the dough for a pie crust in advance. To do so, follow the steps through dividing the dough into 2 balls. Place the dough balls in a mixing bowl, cover tightly with a lid, and store in the refrigerator overnight.

Key Lime Pie

Key Lime Pie is a classic crowd pleaser. Its tart citrus custard is a light, but sweet-tooth satiating, dessert that calls to mind the slow pace of summer dinners on the deck or ocean breezes on an island vacation.

YIELD: 1 (8-inch [20-cm]) pie

- 3 tablespoons cornstarch
- ¾ cup (150 g) organic granulated cane sugar
- 1¼ cups (296 mL) water
- ½ cup (117 g) silken tofu, drained for 30 minutes on a paper towel or cheesecloth
- 2 teaspoons canola oil
- Pinch sea salt
- ½ recipe Homemade Pie Crust (see recipe on p. 161)
- ¼ cup (59 mL) Key lime juice
- Zest of 1 lime
- Vegan whipped cream, for topping

1. In a small mixing bowl, whisk together the cornstarch and sugar, making a dry slurry. Set aside.

2. In the bowl of a food processor fitted with the metal "S" blade, combine the water, tofu, oil, and salt and process until smooth.

3. Pour the cornstarch–sugar slurry into the bowl of the food processor and process until fully combined.

4. Prepare the Homemade Pie Crust recipe, using only ½ the ingredients, through Step 7, since you will be preparing only 1 crust, rather than 2 (this is a single-crust pie).

5. Preheat the oven to 350°F (180°C).

6. Transfer the mixture in the food processor to a medium saucepan over medium heat. Bring to a boil, whisking constantly. Remove from the heat. Add the lime juice and zest and stir well.

7. Pour the contents of the saucepan into the prepared pie crust and bake for 8 to 10 minutes, until the filling sets up. You do not want the filling to bubble, so keep an eye on it throughout the baking time. Remove from the oven.

8. Cool on a wire rack at room temperature until cool to the touch. Refrigerate for 4 to 6 hours to set up. Slice and serve, topped with the vegan whipped cream.

BAKERS' NOTE: This pie is ideally prepared the day before it is to be served and refrigerated overnight.

Strawberry Rhubarb Pie

Rhubarb is a perennial root vegetable commonly found in the Midwest. Its tartness pairs perfectly with the sweetness of midsummer berries like strawberries. The combination of flavors evokes a sense of summer gatherings and cookouts.

YIELD: **1 (8-inch [20-cm]) pie**

- 3 cups (498 g) fresh strawberries, sliced
- 3 cups (366 g) rhubarb, sliced
- ½ cup (100 g) organic granulated cane sugar
- ½ cup (113 g) organic light brown sugar
- ½ tablespoon fresh lemon juice
- Zest of 1 lemon
- 1 recipe Homemade Pie Crust (see recipe on p. 161)
- 4 tablespoons (¼ cup or 30 g) cornstarch, divided
- 2 tablespoons melted vegan margarine, for brushing (optional)

1. In a large mixing bowl, combine the strawberries, rhubarb, sugars, lemon juice, and zest, and let rest for 30 minutes. Drain, reserving the liquid in a small mixing bowl, and set aside.

2. Preheat the oven to 325°F (160°C). Prepare the Homemade Pie Crust recipe through Step 7. Set aside.

3. Add 2 tablespoons of the cornstarch to the reserved liquid and mix well, creating a slurry.

4. Transfer the slurry to a small saucepan over medium-high heat. Cook, stirring frequently, for 10 minutes, until the mixture just comes to a boil.

5. Reduce the heat to low and simmer, stirring constantly with a spoon, for 7 to 9 minutes, until the fruit syrup is thick enough to coat the back of the spoon. Pay close attention as it cooks, as the mixture can burn very easily. Remove from the heat.

6. To the mixing bowl containing the fruit, add the remaining 2 tablespoons of cornstarch and mix well.

7. Place the fruit mixture in the prepared pie crust. Pour the fruit syrup over the fruit.

8. To transfer the top crust to the pie, curl it slightly over the rolling pin. Center it over the pie plate and drape it over.

9. Fold the excess dough over the edge of the pie plate. Pinch the edges of the top crust into the edges of the bottom crust to seal it, or use a fork. Slice 3 holes in the center of the top crust to vent while baking. Brush the top with the vegan margarine to aid in browning the crust, if using.

10. Bake for 40 minutes, until the crust is golden and the pie is set and bubbling a bit at the edges. Remove from the oven and let cool at room temperature for 20 minutes. Slice and serve.

BAKERS' NOTES: 1 stalk rhubarb yields about 1 cup (122 g) sliced.

Consider doing a lattice top for this pie. Make the Homemade Pie Crust recipe as specified, but after rolling out the top crust, cut it into strips and lay the strips over the pie in a crisscross pattern.

Mickey's SOS Oatmeal Cookies

On her constant quest to eat as healthy as she can while still enjoying life's indulgences, Jo created these sugar-free, oil-free, and salt-free cookies. They are one of Mickey's favorites because they satisfy a dessert craving without blowing a diet.

YIELD: **24 cookies**

- ⅓ cup (46 g) raw cashews or ½ cup (119 mL) applesauce
- 6–8 medjool dates, pitted
- ½ banana
- ¾–1 cup (178–237 mL) water
- Juice of 1 large orange
- 1 teaspoon pure vanilla extract
- 1 cup (158 g) oat or rice flour
- 3 tablespoons (42 g) milled flaxseed
- 1½ teaspoons ground cinnamon
- ¾ teaspoon baking soda
- ¾ teaspoon baking powder
- ½ teaspoon ground nutmeg
- Zest of 1 orange
- 2 cups (180 g) quick-cooking oats
- ¾ cup (123 g) raisins
- ½ cup (50 g) walnuts (optional)

1. In a small mixing bowl, cover the cashews and dates (or just the dates if you are using applesauce in place of the cashews) in water. Soak for 30 minutes. Drain.

2. Preheat the oven to 350°F (180°C). Line 2 baking sheets with parchment paper.

3. In a blender or the bowl of a food processor fitted with the metal "S" blade, place the soaked nuts or applesauce, dates, banana, ¾ cup (178 mL) water, orange juice, and vanilla extract and process until combined. If the mixture seems too dry, add the remaining ¼ cup (59 mL) water and process again.

4. In a large mixing bowl, sift together the flour, flaxseed, cinnamon, baking soda, baking powder, and nutmeg. Add the orange zest and stir to combine.

5. Stir the nut and date mixture into the flour mixture. Add the oats, raisins, and walnuts (if using) and stir to combine.

6. Using a small ice cream scoop, form balls in the dough and place them onto the prepared baking sheets. Bake for 10 to 12 minutes. Remove from the oven. Cool on a wire rack and serve.

BAKERS' NOTE: It's no problem to make these cookies gluten free—just use gluten-free oats. But the quick-cooking oats definitely work better in this recipe.

Press lightly with damp fingertips, because these are more dense than regular cookies.

VARIATION: If you prefer your cookies a bit sweeter, replace the water with natural, unsweetened apple juice. You can also add a pinch of salt if you're not on a low-salt diet and want them to have the punch salt gives baked goods.

Snickerdoodle Cookies

The snickerdoodle is a classic cookie. Its cinnamon sugar simplicity is really tough to beat. If made properly, these cookies have just the right amount of chewiness.

YIELD: **20 cookies, each 2 inches (5 cm) in diameter**

For the Cinnamon Sugar:

- ½ **cup (100 g) organic granulated cane sugar**
- ¼–½ **teaspoon ground cinnamon**

For the Cookies:

- 2 **cups (242 g) + 1½ tablespoons unbleached organic all-purpose flour**
- ¾ **teaspoon baking soda**
- ½ **teaspoon sea salt**
- 1 **cup (200 g) + 2½ tablespoons organic granulated cane sugar**
- ½ **cup (112 g) + ½ tablespoon vegan margarine (we like Earth Balance)**
- 1 **teaspoon pure vanilla extract**
- ¼ **cup (59 mL) warm water**

To make the Cinnamon Sugar:

1. In a small mixing bowl, stir together the sugar and cinnamon. Set aside.

To make the Cookies:

1. Preheat the oven to 350°F (180°C). Line 2 baking sheets with parchment paper.

2. In a large mixing bowl, sift together the flour, baking soda, and salt. Set aside.

3. Using a stand mixer fitted with the paddle attachment, cream together the sugar and vegan margarine on high speed for 2 to 3 minutes, until fluffy. Be sure to scrape the sides of the bowl occasionally during the creaming process.

4. Reduce the mixer speed to low and gradually add the vanilla extract and water. Raise the mixer speed to medium and continue mixing until no signs of the water remain.

5. Reduce the mixer speed to low and gradually add the flour mixture in thirds. Turn off the mixer and remove the bowl.

6. Using a small ice cream scoop, form balls in the dough. Roll each ball in the Cinnamon Sugar and place each on the prepared baking sheets.

7. Bake for 10 to 15 minutes, until golden brown. Remove from the oven. Allow the cookies to cool on a wire rack. Serve immediately or store in an airtight container for up to 7 days.

VARIATION: To turn these into Chocolate Chip Cookies, fold in ¾ cup (135 g) dairy-free semisweet chocolate chips at the end of the mixing process and skip the roll in the Cinnamon Sugar.

Molasses Sugar Cookies

These molasses- and ginger-spiced cookies are perfect for the holiday season or for a late-night treat by the fire on a snowy winter night.

YIELD: **2 dozen cookies**

- ¾ cup (178 mL) melted vegan shortening
- 1 cup (200 g) + 2 tablespoons organic granulated cane sugar, divided
- ¼ cup (59 mL) molasses
- ¼ cup (59 mL) soy milk
- 2¼ cups (304 g) whole wheat flour
- 2 teaspoons baking soda
- 1 teaspoon ground cinnamon
- ½ teaspoon ground cloves
- ½ teaspoon ground ginger
- ½ teaspoon sea salt

1. Allow the shortening to cool to room temperature and place it in a medium mixing bowl. Add the 1 cup (200 g) sugar, molasses, and soy milk and beat well with a whisk.

2. In a large mixing bowl, sift together the flour, baking soda, cinnamon, cloves, ginger, and salt.

3. Pour the wet ingredients into the dry ingredients, mixing well. Refrigerate for 1 to 4 hours.

4. Preheat the oven to 375°F (190°C). Line 2 baking sheets with parchment paper.

5. Let the dough sit on counter for 15 minutes to soften a bit. On a clean, lightly floured work surface, form the dough into 1-inch (2.5-cm) balls using a small ice cream scoop and flatten them slightly with your palms. Place the dough balls on the prepared baking sheets and sprinkle them with sugar.

6. Bake for 8 to 10 minutes. Remove from the oven and place on a wire rack to cool. Serve.

BAKERS' NOTE: When working with parchment paper, sprinkle a little water on your work surface to help keep it in place.

VARIATION: To make Sugar Cookies, omit the molasses, cloves, and ginger and add 1½ teaspoons pure vanilla extract and 1½ teaspoons orange zest to the wet ingredient mixture.

Chicago Diner Vegan Milkshake

Our vegan milkshakes helped put us on the map, and now you can make these illustrious vegan milkshakes right in your home kitchen.

YIELD: **2 cups (474 mL)**

- **1½ cups (210 g) vegan ice cream (vanilla, chocolate, or cookie dough flavor)**
- **½ cup (119 mL) soy milk, or more if needed**
- **Vegan whipped cream and a House Cherry (see recipe on p. 56), for topping (optional)**

1. Place the vegan ice cream and soy milk in a blender. Blend until the shake reaches a nice, thick consistency. Add more soy milk, if necessary. Pour into a tall glass and top with the vegan whipped cream and House Cherry. Serve immediately.

VARIATION: To turn this shake into a Strawberry Sensation, start with ½ cup (83 g) frozen strawberries. Add soy milk to cover and blend the mixture a bit. Last, add ¾ (105 g) cup vegan vanilla ice cream.

To make a Peanut Butter Shake, simply add 1 tablespoon peanut butter to the standard shake recipe.

Try pulsing in chocolate chips, toasted nuts, crunchy cookies and other fun things for a few seconds after the shake is fully blended. It adds wonderful crunch and flavor.

Index

L

M

N

O

P

Q

R

S

T

U

V

W

Y

Z

Acknowledgments

JO A. KAUCHER

Thank you …

- To my mother and family, for sharing a love of good food and healthy eating with me.
- To our staff, for all the great contributions and for sharing their creativity and talents over many years.
- To our kitchen crew, bakers, family and friends for testing and tasting recipe conversions, as well as giving me your upbeat support.
- To Del, for his beautiful photos, writing skills, hard work, and being our all around tech-savvy guy.
- To Kat, for your positive, organized, and colorful hard work and energies, and for bringing the book to fruition.
- To Shirley, for your wonderful food styling; your hard work is sincerely appreciated.
- To my loving husband Mickey; I give him very special thanks for his patience, understanding, and humor. Thank you for being my guinea pig and for your great taste.
- To Michael, our general manager and loving nephew; thanks for joining us, and for sharing your people skills, your strong sense of business, and your calm amidst the fire.
- To our wonderful customers; it is my life's pleasure to have helped provide tens of thousands of vegetarian meals for your enjoyment and health.
- To the many conscientious animal and social justice organizations that have lent their mutual support to our efforts.
- To the veggie community, both local and throughout the country; you have all helped us and have worked together to make a meat-free diet available to our society.
- To Eileen Johnson, Perrin Davis, and Doug Seibold, for your patience, high-quality work, and perseverance with deadlines.

KAT BARRY

First and foremost, I want to thank my parents for their endless support and encouragement, especially during these last few years. I extend my deepest gratitude to all the women who raised me and showed me the power and beauty of knowing your way around the kitchen and the fulfillment in feeding those you love. Thank you to my closest kitchen-goddess friends—Khaylen, Courtney, and Jill—for sending me recipes, sharing your knowledge, and helping me heal through food. I also give thanks to my Aunt Laura, for taking the vegan plunge with me and changing my life forever; to my brilliant big brothers, Mick and Dave, for always being my heroes; to Larry Schuler and Brett Boyd, who gave me a chance; to Steven Welsh for helping with everything from getting "camera ready" to washing radishes; and to our amazing publishers, Eileen Johnson, Perrin Davis, and Doug Seibold.

I want to extend a special thank you to Mickey and Jo for making me a part of the Diner team and for giving me this opportunity, believing in me, and trusting me. I've learned so much from both of you, and I cannot thank you enough. Jo, I cherish the hours we spent in the dining room on Halsted going over recipes and brainstorming about food. I give thanks as well to all my coworkers at the Chicago Diner who contributed to this book and who make going to work every day so much fun. I give special thanks to Del, who has devoted countless hours working on this project and with whom I work closely every day.

Last, I want to dedicate my contribution to this book to my incredible grandmother, Inez, who died while we were writing this manuscript. As a former home-ec teacher, cook, and lover of salad, she was a true inspiration to me in the in kitchen and in life, and I know she would be very proud.

JAMESON

About the Authors

JO A. KAUCHER, a Chicago native and self-taught chef, learned the tricks of the trade as an experienced cook and baker in restaurant and hotel kitchens. She became vegetarian in 1971 and hasn't looked back. In 1983, she co-founded the meat-free Chicago Diner, pioneering the combination of vegetarian cuisine with comfort food flair.

Michigan native, self-made chef, media-savvy personality, and founder of her own catering business, **KAT BARRY** became vegan in 2007. Because plant-based living so profoundly improved her health, she is now passionately committed to educating and inspiring others to do the same.